EXERCISES FOR

Ellsworth/Higgins

ENGLISH
SIMPLIFIED

Eleventh Edition

Bruce Thaler

PEARSON
Longman

New York   Boston   San Francisco
London   Toronto   Sydney   Tokyo   Singapore   Madrid
Mexico City   Munich   Paris   Cape Town   Hong Kong   Montreal

Acquisitions Editor: Melanie Craig
Senior Supplements Editor: Donna Campion
Electronic Page Makeup: Dianne Hall

Exercises for Ellsworth/Higgins, *English Simplified,* Eleventh Edition

ISBN: 0-321-42933-8

2 3 4 5 6 7 8 9 10–BRR–09 08 07

CONTENTS

(ESL denotes that the exercise has an ESL component. C denotes choice-type items; W denotes items asking for original written responses.)

PREFACE

The eleventh edition of *Exercises for English Simplified* provides instructors with two types of exercises for assessing and developing students' writing and researching skills. For instructors who want quick, easy scoring, there are nearly three thousand choice-type items (exercises including these are labeled C in the table of contents). For instructors who prefer original, open-ended responses, there are hundreds of items for which students compose their own answers—words, sentences, paragraphs, even a full essay (exercises including these are labeled W in the table of contents).

The eleventh edition retains the extensive revisions of the tenth, with further improvements including

- Numbering of the five parts of the book, with section numbers within each part beginning with that part number—part 1 covering sections 101-130, part 2 sections 201-227, and so forth; this prevents confusion between section numbers and page numbers

- New exercise items to address the addition of a new section, "A Word Group as a Part of Speech"

- Although the Columbia Online Style (COS) has been dropped from the research section of the eleventh edition (a note refers students to the COS website), for times when instructors specify the COS alternative, the Answer Key includes answers using the COS form.

Revisions retained from the tenth edition include

- Updated research exercises reflecting the latest MLA and APA form revisions, and including evaluation of sources

- An expanded exercise on note-taking, avoiding plagiarism, and citing

- A new exercise on online writing

- A more legible Answer Key format for easier scoring

Longman Publishers wishes to acknowledge the expert advice offered by the following during the revision of *Exercises for English Simplified:* Jeff Andelora, Mesa Community College; Dr. Eileen Ariza, Florida Atlantic University; Christine Gray, Community College of Baltimore County; Rita Hamada-Kahn, Cal Poly Pomona; Kristen Holland, Franklin University; Dr. Carol A. Lenhart, Arizona Western College; David Siar, Winston Salem State University; and Stephen A. Smolen, Saddleback College.

1. DIAGNOSTIC TEST: Sentences, Grammar, and Paragraphs

Part 1: Sentences

In the blank after each sentence,

Write **S** if the boldfaced expression is **one complete, correct sentence.**
Write **F** if it is a **fragment** (incorrect: less than a complete sentence).
Write **R** if it is a **run-on** (incorrect: two or more sentences written as one—also known as a **comma splice** or **fused sentence**).

Example: The climbers suffered from hypothermia. **Having neglected to bring warm clothing.**　　　　___F___

1. State inspectors have found doctors-in-training at State Hospital working excessive hours. **However, the hospital has promised to reduce their work load at once.**　　1._____

2. The bank's computers have broken down again. **All transactions halted, and hundreds of customers angry.**　　2._____

3. **In Russia, pork is sold for 465 rubles a pound that amount is equivalent to the average monthly salary.**　　3._____

4. The Yankees made two big trades after the season had begun. **First for a shortstop and then for a center fielder.**　　4._____

5. The African American Society put Martina Jones in charge of the Multicultural Festival. **A responsibility that appealed to her.**　　5._____

6. **The boys are learning traditional Irish dancing, they really seem to enjoy their dance class.**　　6._____

7. The President eventually seemed happy to retire from politics. **His family looking forward to spending more time with him.**　　7._____

8. **Although American society may seem uncaring, more people are volunteering to help with the homeless.**　　8._____

9. **The reason for her shyness being that she knew no one at the party except her hostess.**　　9._____

10. **The experiment to produce nuclear fusion was both controversial and exciting, scientists all over the world attempted to duplicate its results.**　　10._____

11. **Scientists have learned that sick bison can infect livestock with a serious bacterial disease.**　　11._____

12. She loved all styles of art. **She said she particularly loved the impressionists, she had studied them in Paris.**　　12._____

13. We walked over to the lost-and-found office. **To see whether the bag had been turned in.**　　13._____

14. **The shift lever must be in neutral only then will the car start.**　　14._____

15. **Buenos Aires, Argentina, is a lively city, the streets are safe at all times.** Movie theaters stay open all night.　　15._____

16. **If you want an unusual form of exercise, learn to play the bagpipes.**　　16._____

In the blank,

Write **C** if the boldfaced expression is used **correctly**.
Write **X** if it is used **incorrectly**.

Example: There **was** dozens of dinosaur bones on the site.   X

1. We need to keep this a secret between you and **I**.   1. _____

2. Bill was fired from his new job, **which** made him despondent.   2. _____

3. Each member will be responsible for **their** own transportation.   3. _____

4. There **was** at least five computers in the office.   4. _____

5. Several of **us** newcomers needed a map to find our way around.   5. _____

6. Every administrator and faculty member **was** required to attend the orientation program.   6. _____

7. The graduate teaching assistant and **myself** met for a review session.   7. _____

8. Surprisingly enough, presidential candidate Joan Smith was leading **not only** in the cities **but also** in the rural areas.   8. _____

9. In each sack lunch **were** a cheese sandwich, an apple, and a soda.   9. _____

10. Leave the message with **whoever** answers the phone.   10. _____

11. **Having made no other plans for the evening,** Tony was glad to accept the invitation.   11. _____

12. Everyone in the Hispanic Society **was** urged to join the movement to bring more Hispanic faculty to campus.   12. _____

13. If I **were** driving to Pennsylvania this weekend, I would take along my sketch pad.   13. _____

14. I bought one of the printers that **were** on sale.   14. _____

15. There **were** five different Asian student organizations on campus.   15. _____

16. The prosecutor demanded that the witness tell her **when did she hear the shot**.   16. _____

17. The director, as well as the choir members, **has** agreed to appear on television.   17. _____

18. The supervisor is especially fond of arranging training programs, working on elaborate projects, and **to develop budgets.**   18. _____

19. A faux pas **is when you commit a social blunder**.   19. _____

20. **Who** do you think mailed the anonymous letter to the editor?   20. _____

21. Neither the students nor the instructor **knows** where the notice is to be posted.   21. _____

22. Are you sure that it was **him** that you saw last evening?   22. _____

23. Between you and **me**, her decision to transfer to another department was not well received by her current supervisor.   23. _____

24. If the dog **had been** on a leash, it would not have been hit by a car.   24. _____

25. He joined the Big Brothers Organization and coached in Little League. **It** was expected of him by his law firm.   25. _____

26. Given the candidates, it's painfully clear that **us** voters didn't have much of a choice.   26 _____

27. Customers should check the fruit carefully before paying; otherwise, **you** may end up with rotten or spoiled fruit.   27. _____

28. Anyone who forgets his book will not be able to take **their** report home   28. _____

29. While carrying my books to the library, **a squirrel darted across my path.**   29. _____

30. Norma **only** had one issue left to raise before she could rest her case.   30. _____

31. I had no idea that **my** giving a report would create such turmoil at the meeting.   31. _____

32. We didn't think that many of **us** substitutes would get into the game.   32. _____

33. Dean Robert Patterson gave Karen and **I** permission to establish a volunteer organization to tutor students from city schools.   33. _____

34. Although he often spoke harshly to others, his voice sounded **pleasant** to us.   34. _____

35. Neither the librarian nor the students in the reference room **was** aware of the situation.   35. _____

36. Professor Rogers looks very **differently** since he dyed his beard and moustache.   36. _____

37. There is no question that it was **she** under the table.   37. _____

38. The audience comprised **not only juniors but also seniors**.   38. _____

39. Dr. Smith, together with thirty of his students, **are** working at a community service site.   39. _____

40. Each of three employees **were** given a set of business cards.   40. _____

41. The only kind of transportation running **are** buses.   41. _____

42. **Standing motionless on the windswept, dreary plain,** the rain pelted my face.   42. _____

43. I had agreed to **promptly and without delay** notify them of my decision.   43. _____

44. The dean agreed to award the scholarship to **whomever** the committee selected.   44. _____

45. **Knowing that I should study**, it seemed important to unplug the phone.   45. _____

46. **Who** were you looking for in the auditorium?   46. _____

47. The noise and the general chaos caused by the alarm **were** disturbing to the visitor.   47. _____

48. As hard as I try, I'll never be as thin as **her**.   48. _____

49. Only one of these stamps **is** of real value.   49. _____

50. Only my brother and **myself** were allowed in after visiting hours.   50. _____

Part 3: Paragraphs (not included in scoring)

On the back of this page, write a **paragraph** of six to eight sentences on **one** of the topics below (you may also use scrap paper):

I will never do *that* again

My room (or clothes, car, etc.) as a reflection of me

If I were mayor (or governor or president) for one day

The best (or worst) film I have seen in the past year

The most unfair law

Name _____ Class _____ Date_____ Score (R____x 1.33) _____

2. DIAGNOSTIC TEST: Punctuation

In the blank after each sentence,

Write **C** if the punctuation in brackets is **correct**;
Write **X** if it is **incorrect**.

(Use only one letter in each blank.)

Example: Regular exercise[,] and sound nutrition are essential for good health.   _____X_____

1. The legislature has voted to close the old County Nursing Home[;] a larger, more modern home will replace it.   1._____

2. "What hope is there that the war will end soon[?]" the ambassador asked.   2._____

3. "Why can't a woman be more like a man["?] the chauvinist asked.   3._____

4. I learned that the newly elected officers were Marzell Brown, president[;] Leroy Jones, vice president[;] Sandra Smith, treasurer[;] and James Chang, secretary.   4._____

5. The class expected low grades[. T]he test having been long and difficult.   5._____

6. It[']s hard to imagine life without a VCR, a personal computer, and a cell phone.   6._____

7. Eventually, everybody comes to Rick's[;] the best saloon in Casablanca.   7._____

8. Recognizing that busing places stress on younger students[,] the state officials are restructuring the school transportation system.   8._____

9. Richard Hernandez was unhappy at his college[,] he missed hearing Spanish and enjoying his favorite foods.   9._____

10. That is not the Sullivans' boat; at least, I think that it isn't their[']s.   10._____

11. When it rains, I always think of the opening lines of Longfellow's poem "The Rainy Day": "The day is cold, and dark, and dreary [/] It rains, and the wind is never weary."   11._____

12. Inspector Trace asked, "Is that all you remember?[" "]Are you sure?"   12._____

13. "The report is ready," Chisholm said[,] "I'm sending it to the supervisor today."   13._____

14. Didn't I hear you say, "I especially like blueberry pie"[?]   14._____

15. Joe enrolled in a small college[;] although he had planned originally to join a rock band.   15._____

16. Stanley moved to Minneapolis[,] where he hoped to open a restaurant.   16._____

17. That was a bit too close for comfort[,] wasn't it?   17._____

18. The advertiser received more than two[-]hundred replies on the Internet.   18._____

19. Sarah is asking for a week[']s vacation to visit relatives in Canada.   19._____

20. On February 21, 2008[,] Robin and Sam are getting married.   20._____

21. The womens['] basketball team has reached the state finals.   21._____

22. Recently, researchers have discovered that rhesus monkeys have some hidden talents[;] such as the ability to do basic math.   22._____

23. She received twenty[-]three greeting cards on her nineteenth birthday.   23._____

24. He caught the pass[,] and dashed for the end zone.

24. _____

25. Many weeks before school was out[;] he had applied for a summer job.

25. _____

26. Dear Sir[;] Please accept this letter of application for the teaching position.

26. _____

27. Schweitzer summed up his ethics as "reverence for life[,]" a phrase that came to him during his early years in Africa.

27. _____

28. Our communications professor asked us if we understood the use of extended periods of silence often found in conversations among Native Americans[?]

28. _____

29. "As for who won the election[—]well, not all the votes have been counted," she said.

29. _____

30. ["]The Perils of Aerobic Dancing["]   (This is the title at the head of a student's essay for an English class.)

30. _____

31. Any music[,] that is not jazz[,] does not appeal to him.

31. _____

32. "Election results are coming in quickly now," the newscaster announced[;] "and we should be able to predict the winner soon."

32. _____

33. More than 42 percent of all adults eighteen and over are single[,] however, more than 90 percent of these adults will marry at least once.

33. _____

34. The children went to the zoo[;] bought ice-cream cones[;] fed peanuts to the elephants[;] and watched the seals perform their tricks while being fed.

34. _____

35. ["]For He's a Jolly Good Fellow["] is my grandfather's favorite song to sing at birthday parties.

35. _____

36. In the early 1900s, department stores provided customers electric lighting, public telephones, and escalators[;] and these stores offered countless other services, such as post offices, branch libraries, root gardens, and in-store radio stations.

36. _____

37. Watch out[,] Marlene, for icy patches on the sidewalk.

37. _____

38. The rival candidates for the Senate are waging an all-out campaign[,] until the polls open tomorrow.

38. _____

39. Because he stayed up to play computer games[,] he didn't make it to his early class.

39. _____

40. The weather[—]rain, rain, and more rain[—]has ruined our weekend plans for an entire month.

40. _____

41. The first modern drive-in was called[,] The Pig Stand, which was a barbecue pit along a highway between Dallas and Fort Worth.

41. _____

42. The scholarship award went to Julia Brown, the student[,] who had the highest grades.

42. _____

43. Some of the technologies developed after World War II were[:] television, synthetic fibers, and air travel.

43. _____

44. The Lincoln Highway[,] which was the first transcontinental highway[,] officially opened in 1923 and was advertised as America's Main Street.

44. _____

45. Esther Greenberg[,] who is my roommate[,] comes from a small town.

45. _____

46. I hav[']ent made up my mind whether I want a computer system with an attached video camera.

46. _____

47. The talk show host[,] irritated and impatient[,] cut off the caller who insisted he was calling from aboard a flying saucer.

47. _____

48. Author Mike Rose writes[:] "When a local public school is lost to incompetence, indifference, or despair, it should be an occasion for mourning. . . ."

48. _____

49. A note under the door read: "Sorry you weren't in. The Emerson[']s."

49. _____

50. Most of my friends are upgrading their computer security systems[,] they want to be safe from computer viruses and identity theft.   50. _____

51. This spring we began a new family vacation tradition[:] we flew to Florida to watch the Indians' spring training.   51. _____

52. No matter how cute they look, squirrels[,] in my opinion[,] are very destructive rodents.   52. _____

53. We are planning a trip to Chicago[,] the children will enjoy the city's museums.   53. _____

54. By saving her money[,] Laura was able to build her cottage on the lake.   54. _____

55. To gain recognition as a speaker[;] he accepted all invitations to appear before civic groups.   55. _____

56. Charles Wright[,] who survived an avalanche in the Himalayas[,] thought he heard a flute just before the storm occurred.   56. _____

57. Any candidate[,] who wants to increase social spending[,] will probably be defeated during the upcoming elections.   57. _____

58. "Oh, well[!]" the officer yawned, "I guess I'll stop in for coffee and a bagel."   58. _____

59. "I cannot believe that you have not read my book!"[,] shouted the author to the critic.   59. _____

60. In his painting [*The Red Dog,*] the French artist Paul Gauguin painted people from Tahiti in a bold and bright style.   60. _____

61. A group of workers in Westerville, Ohio[,] won a multi-million dollar lottery prize.   61. _____

62. According to my family's written records, my great-grandfather was born in 1870[,] and died in 1895.   62. _____

63. My hometown is a place[,] where older men still think white shoes and belts are high fashion.   63. _____

64. She spent her student teaching practicum in Johnstown[,] where she went to hockey games each week.   64. _____

65. Having learned that she was eligible for a scholarship[,] she turned in her application.   65. _____

66. Living in his car for three weeks[,] did not especially bother him.   66. _____

67. The novel ["Underworld"] uses a famous home-run baseball as both a symbol and a unifying device.   67. _____

68. Many Americans remember family celebrations from their childhood[,] moreover, they are seeking ways to incorporate some of these rituals into their busy lives.   68. _____

69. In 1888 a bank clerk named George Eastman created the first amateur camera, called the Detective Camera[;] this camera was a small black box with a button and a key for advancing the film.   69. _____

70. After the long, harsh winter, I needed a soak[-]in[-]the[-]sun vacation.   70. _____

71. Veterans of World War I[,] who were hit hard by the Great Depression[,] received a government bonus in the 1930s.   71. _____

72. The girls['] and boys['] locker rooms had no heat.   72. _____

73. The parking lot always is full[,] when there is a concert.   73. _____

74. Dan was proud that he received all *A*[']s.   74. _____

75. You can reach Delaware Avenue by turning left[,] and following Route 19.   75. _____

3. DIAGNOSTIC TEST: Mechanics, Spelling, and Word Choice

Part 1: Capitalization

In each blank, write **C** if the boldfaced word(s) **follow** the rules of capitalization.
Write **X** if the word(s) **do not follow** the rules.

Example: The Mormons settled in what is now Salt Lake **City**.   _C_

1. The *Andrea Doria* sank in the 1950s.   1. ____
2. My **college** days were stressful.   2. ____
3. He attends Taft **high school.**   3. ____
4. The **President** vetoed the bill.   4. ____
5. They drove **east** from Tucson.   5. ____
6. We presented **Mother** with a bouquet of roses.   6. ____
7. I finally passed **spanish**.   7. ____
8. She is in France; **He** is at home.   8. ____
9. "Are you working?" **she** asked.   9. ____
10. I love **Korean** food.   10. ____

11. We saluted the **american** flag.   11. ____
12. Last **Summer** I drove to California.   12. ____
13. My birthday was **Friday**.   13. ____
14. I am enrolled in courses in **philosophy** and Japanese.   14. ____
15. She went **North** for Christmas.   15. ____
16. Please, **Father**, lend me your car.   16. ____
17. "But he's my **Brother**," she wailed.   17. ____
18. "Stop!" **shouted** the officer.   18. ____
19. Jane refused to be **Chairperson** of the committee.   19. ____
20. "If possible," he said, "**Write** the report today."   20. ____

Part 2: Abbreviations and Numbers

Write **C** if the boldfaced abbreviation or number is used **correctly**.
Write **X** it is used **incorrectly**.

Example: They drove through **Tenn.**   _X_

1. **Six billion** people now inhabit the world.   1. ____
2. I participated in a **five-hour** workshop on interpersonal communications.   2. ____
3. The play begins at **7** p.m.   3. ____
4. Aaron was born on November **11th,** 1988.   4. ____
5. The rent is **$325** a month.   5. ____
6. The interest comes to **8** percent.   6. ____
7. **Sen.** Levy voted against the bill.   7. ____
8. There are **nineteen** women in the club.   8. ____

9. **2005** was another bad year for flooding.   9. ____
10. I wrote a note to **Dr**. Rhee.   10. ____
11. [Opening sentence of a news article] The **ACDYM** has filed for bankruptcy.   11. ____
12. She lives on Buchanan **Ave**.   12. ____
13. We consulted Ricardo Guitierrez, **Ph.D.**   13. ____
14. Our appointment is at **4** o'clock.   14. ____
15. I slept only **3** hours last night.   15. ____

Part 3: Spelling

In each sentence, one boldfaced word is **misspelled.** Write its number in the blank.

Example: (1)**Its** (2)**too** late (3)**to** go.   ___1___

1. Jane's (1)**independent** attitude sometimes was a (2)**hindrence** to the (3)**committee**.   1. _____

2. (1)**Approximatly** half of the class noticed the (2)**omission** of the last item on the (3)**questionnaire**.   2. _____

3. The (1)**mischievous** child was (2)**usualy** (3)**courteous** to adults.   3. _____

4. At the office Jack was described as an (1)**unusually** (2)**conscientous** and (3)**indispensable** staff member.   4. _____

5. Even though Dave was (1)**competent** in his (2)**mathematics** class, he didn't have the (3)**disipline** required to work through the daily homework.   5. _____

6. The sociologist's (1)**analysis** of the (2)**apparent** (3)**prejudise** that existed among the villagers was insightful.   6. _____

7. She was (1)**particularly** (2)**sensable** about maintaining a study (3)**schedule**.   7. _____

8. It was (1)**necesary** to curb Tad's (2)**tendency** to interrupt the staff discussion with (3)**irrelevant** comments.   8. _____

9. (1)**Personaly**, it was no (2)**surprise** that (3)**curiosity** prompted the toddler to smear lipstick on the bathroom mirror.   9. _____

10. Tim developed a (1)**procedure** for updating our (2)**bussiness** (3)**calendar**.   10. _____

11. As a (1)**sophomore** Sue had the (2)**perseverence** and (3)**sacrifice** needed to work three part-time jobs and to raise her three sons.   11. _____

12. Her (1)**opinion**, while (2)**fascinating**, revealed an indisputable (3)**hypocricy**.   12. _____

13. Every day our (1)**secretery** meets a colleague from the (2)**Psychology** Department at their favorite campus (3)**restaurant**.   13. _____

14. During (1)**adolescence** we often (2)**condemm** anyone who offers (3)**guidance**.   14. _____

15. Based on Bill's (1)**description**, his dream vacation sounded (2)**irresistable** and guaranteed to (3)**fulfill** anyone's need to escape.   15. _____

Part 4: Word Choice

To be correct, the boldfaced expression must be standard, formal English and must not be sexist or otherwise discriminatory.

Write **C** if the boldfaced word is used **correctly**.
Write **X** if it is used **incorrectly**.

Examples: The counsel's **advice** was misinterpreted. __C__

They **could of** made the plane except for the traffic. __X__

1. Her car is different **than** mine.   1. ____

2. He **hadn't hardly** any chance.   2. ____

3. The plane began its **descent** for Denver.   3. ____

4. Economic problems always **impact** our enrollment.   4. ____

5. My glasses **lay** where I had put them.   5. ____

6. We didn't play **good** in the last quarter.   6. ____

10

7. I selected a **nice** birthday card. 7. ____

8. The float **preceded** the band in the parade. 8. ____

9. No one predicted the **affects** of the bomb. 9. ____

10. My aunt always uses unusual **stationery**. 10. ____

11. I dislike **those kind** of cookies. 11. ____

12. We are going to **canvas** the school district for the scholarship fund. 12. ____

13. The computer **sits** on a small table. 13. ____

14. College men and **girls** are warned not to drink and drive. 14. ____

15. The **principal** spoke to the students. 15. ____

16. I **had ought** to learn to use that software. 16. ____

17. He made **less** mistakes than I did. 17. ____

18. The family **better** repair the furnace. 18. ____

19. The package had **burst** open. 19. ____

20. Mrs. Grundy **censured** so much of the play that it was unintelligible. 20. ____

21. We are taught to consider the feelings of our **fellow man**. 21. ____

22. **Irregardless** of the warning, I drove in the dense fog. 22. ____

23. The next **thing** in my argument concerns my opponent's honesty. 23. ____

24. The new carpet **complements** the living room furniture. 24. ____

25. A different **individual** will have to chair the service project. 25. ____

26. I **ought to of** made the flight arrangements. 26. ____

27. **Numerical statistical figures** show that an asteroid may collide with Earth. 27. ____

28. **Due to the fact that** it rained, the game was canceled. 28. ____

29. **That sort of** person is out of place in this salon. 29. ____

30. The parade float was **round in shape**. 30. ____

4. SENTENCES AND GRAMMAR: Parts of a Sentence

(Study 101–103, The Sentence and Its Parts)

Part 1

In the blank, write the number of the place where the **complete subject** ends and the (**complete**) **predicate** begins.

Example: Immigrants (1) to the United States (2) have helped greatly (3) in building the country.   ___2___

1. A new convention center (1) will be constructed (2) on North Main Street (3) within five years.   1._____

2. Many of the abandoned railroad stations (1) of America and Canada (2) have been restored (3) for other uses.   2._____

3. The junction (1) of the Allegheny (2) and Monongahela rivers (3) creates (4) the Ohio River.   3._____

4. The editor (1) wrote a kind note (2) after the long list of changes (3) to be made before final printing.   4._____

5. The United States, (1) Mexico, (2) and Canada (3) now have (4) a free-trade agreement.   5._____

6. I (1) recently completed (2) a twenty-page research paper (3) on the new common currency for European countries.   6._____

7. Which (1) of the three word-processing software packages (2) has (3) the best thesaurus?   7._____

8. Rarely would she drive her car after the earthquakes.
   [This inverted-word-order sentence, rewritten in subject-predicate order, becomes:
   She (1) would rarely (2) drive (3) her car (4) after the earthquakes.]   8._____

9. None (1) of the polls (2) shows Stanton (3) winning.   9._____

10. When did the committee select the candidate for comptroller?
    [Rewritten in subject-predicate order:
    The committee (1) did select (2) the candidate (3) for comptroller when?]   10._____

Part 2

Write **S** if the boldfaced word is a **subject** (or part of a compound subject).
Write **V** if it is a **verb**.
Write **C** if it is a **complement** (or part of a compound complement).

Examples: Wendell played a superb game.   ___S___

Wendell **played** a superb game.   ___V___

Wendell played a superb **game**.   ___C___

1. **Many** paid their taxes late.   1._____

2. Many paid their **taxes** late.   2._____

3. Champion athletes **spend** much time training and competing.   3._____

4. Champion athletes spend much **time** training and competing.   4. _____

5. **Sue** and Janet enjoy gardening.   5. _____

6. Sue and Janet enjoy **gardening**.   6. _____

7. Many **athletes** worry about life after the pros.   7. _____

8. Many athletes **worry** about life after the pros.   8. _____

9. The populist **theme** from the last election may survive until the next election.   9. _____

10. The populist theme from the last election **may survive** until the next election.   10. _____

11. The **neighborhood** worked hard to clean up the local playground.   11. _____

12. The neighborhood **worked** hard to clean up the local playground.   12. _____

13. The clustered lights far below the plane were **cities**.   13. _____

Part 3

In each sentence, fill in the blank with a word of your own that makes sense. Then, in the blank at the right, tell whether it is a **subject** (write **S**), **verb** (write **V**), or **complement** (write **C**).

Example: The builders needed a <u>ladder</u> for the new job.   ___C___

1. Beautiful _____ grow in our garden.   1. _____

2. We grow beautiful _____ in our garden.   2. _____

3. Cabbages, onions, and _____ grow in our garden.   3. _____

4. Three students in English 101 _____ their final examination.   4. _____

5. The instructor was a _____.   5. _____

6. With the ball on the ten-yard line, the crowd _____.   6. _____

7. Shaw wrote a _____ about a speech professor and an uneducated young woman.   7. _____

8. The crisp, clear _____ refreshed us.   8. _____

9. Too many people in this country _____ unconcerned about their health.   9. _____

10. Materials necessary for this course include a(n) _____ and a calculator.   10. _____

5. SENTENCES AND GRAMMAR: Parts of Speech

(Study 104–110, The Parts of Speech)

Write the **part of speech** of each boldfaced word (use the abbreviations in parentheses):

noun	adjective (**adj**)	preposition (**prep**)
pronoun (**pro**)	adverb (**adv**)	conjunction (**conj**)
verb		interjection (**inter**)

Example: Shaw wrote many **plays**.   <u>noun</u>

1. This device is a **modem**.   1. ____

2. Applicants must **complete** this form.   2. ____

3. **She** anticipated the vote.   3. ____

4. The fires caused **many** to flee.   4. ____

5. Robert felt **tired**.   5. ____

6. She has been **there** before.   6. ____

7. The **primary** goal is to reduce spending.   7. ____

8. The test was hard **but** fair.   8. ____

9. Do you want fries **with** that?   9. ____

10. **That** player is going to be a star.   10. ____

11. **That** is not what I meant.   11. ____

12. You are going **beyond** the rules.   12. ____

13. Is this **your** book?   13. ____

14. The book is **mine**.   14. ____

15. He wants an **education**.   15. ____

16. **Wow**, what a shot that was!   16. ____

17. He agreed to proceed **slowly**.   17. ____

18. They **were sleeping** soundly at noon.   18. ____

19. The candidate selected a **charismatic** running mate.   19. ____

20. She is **unusually** talented.   20. ____

21. **Everyone** joined in the protest.   21. ____

22. Auto workers **are striking** for better pay.   22. ____

23. This is the first major **strike** in several years.   23. ____

24. The workers took a **strike** vote.   24. ____

25. He is the one **whom** I suspect.   25. ____

26. The researcher played a video game **while** waiting for the results.   26. ____

27. What is your **plan**?   27. ____

28. Nancy **is** a feminist.   28. ____

29. No one came **after** ten o'clock.   29. ____

30. Put the book **there**.   30. ____

31. I saw him **once**.   31. ____

32. The **theater** was dark.   32. ____

33. The tribe owns a **factory**.   33. ____

34. Weren't **you** surprised?   34. ____

35. They waited **for** us.   35. ____

36. The vote on the motion was quite **close**.   36. ____

37. Did you pay your **dues**?   37. ____

38. **All** survivors were calm.   38. ____

39. **All** were calm.   39. ____

40. The student read **quickly**.   40. ____

41. She **became** an executive.   41. ____

42. **Well**, what shall we do now?   42. ____

43. He worked **during** the summer.   43. ____

44. **Tomorrow** is her birthday.   44. ____

45. Will she call **tomorrow**?   45. ____

46. **If** I go, will you come?   46. ____

47. The executive stood **behind** her staff.   47. ____

48. He should never **have been advanced** in rank.   48. ____

49. The **wild** party was finally over.   49. ____

50. The corporation reported earnings **falsely**.   50. ____

6. SENTENCES AND GRAMMAR: Parts of Speech

(Study 104–110, The Parts of Speech)

Part 1

In the first blank in each sentence, write a word or word group of your own that **makes sense**.
Then in the blank at the right, tell what **part of speech** your word or word group is (use the abbreviations in parentheses):

noun	adjective (**adj**)	preposition (**prep**)
pronoun (**pro**)	adverb (**adv**)	conjunction (**conj**)
verb		interjection (**inter**)

Example: The singer wore a *gaudy* jacket.   ___adj___

(Collaborative option: Students work in pairs, alternating: one writes the word or word group, the other names the part of speech.)

1. The letter should arrive _____.   1. _____
2. May I _____ you Friday?   2. _____
3. Every night, _____ monsters filled his dreams.   3. _____
4. _____ seemed courageous to us.   4. _____
5. Is _____ your locker?   5. _____
6. The _____ was deathly quiet.   6. _____
7. _____ vacation proved quite hazardous.   7. _____
8. _____! I dropped my keys down the sewer.   8. _____
9. Many _____ trees are threatened by acid rain.   9. _____
10. This plane goes _____ Cleveland.   10. _____
11. This is the address _____.   11. _____
12. _____ now.   12. _____
13. They put the motion to a vote, but _____ failed.   13. _____
14. Ms. Kostas _____ a registered pharmacist.   14. _____
15. The senator would _____ accept a bribe.   15. _____
16. Approach that pit bull dog _____ carefully.   16. _____
17. Arles is in France, _____ Aachen is in Germany.   17. _____
18. The jury found that she was _____.   18. _____
19. _____ he won the lottery, he was envied.   19. _____
20. _____ of the runners collapsed from the heat.   20. _____
21. Farnsworth sought refuge _____ the storm.   21. _____
22. Martin was spending his money _____.   22. _____
23. The hill folk have always _____ the valley folk.   23. _____

24. Over the mountains and _____ the woods they trekked.   24. _____

25. _____! That's a sweet-looking car.   25. _____

Part 2

In each blank, write the **correct** preposition: **at**, **in**, or **on**.
(In some blanks, either of two prepositions may be correct.)

Example: Franko lives <u>in</u> an apartment <u>on</u> Broadway.

Fran Bradley, a retired banker, lived _____ a pleasant street _____ a small town _____ the Midwest. Most mornings she awakened promptly _____ six, except _____ Sundays, when she slept until eight. Then she would ride to worship _____ her 1987 Ford or _____ her old three-speed bicycle. Often she was the first one _____ her house of worship.

7. SENTENCES AND GRAMMAR: Uses of Nouns

(Study 112, Using Nouns)

Part 1

In the blank, tell how the boldfaced word in each sentence is **used** (use the abbreviations in parentheses):

subject (**subj**)	indirect object (**ind obj**)	appositive (**app**)
subjective complement (**subj comp**)	objective complement (**obj comp**)	direct address (**dir add**)
direct object (**dir obj**)	object of preposition (**obj prep**)	

Example: The passenger gave the **driver** a tip.   ___ind obj___

1. The **delegates** gathered for the vote.   1. _____
2. The delegates gathered for the **vote**.   2. _____
3. The **committee** named Kamura treasurer.   3. _____
4. The committee named **Kamura** treasurer.   4. _____
5. The committee named Kamura **treasurer**.   5. _____
6. Russo will be a **member** of the board.   6. _____
7. Fallen leaves covered the **path**.   7. _____
8. **Ladies** and gentlemen, here is the star of tonight's show.   8. _____
9. Ladies and gentlemen, here is the **star** of tonight's show.   9. _____
10. The young star, **Leslie Mahoud**, appeared nervous.   10. _____
11. Antilock brakes give the **driver** more control.   11. _____
12. These brakes have become a **source** of controversy.   12. _____
13. These brakes have become a source of **controversy**.   13. _____
14. Misapplication of these brakes has caused some **accidents**.   14. _____
15. Which **company** will get the contract?   15. _____
16. Which company will get the **contract**?   16. _____
17. Everyone was bored by the speaker's **redundancy**.   17. _____
18. Redundancy, needless **repetition**, can put an audience to sleep.   18. _____
19. Marie, make that **customer** an offer she cannot refuse.   19. _____
20. **Marie**, make that customer an offer she cannot refuse.   20. _____
21. The company named Marie **salesperson** of the month.   21. _____
22. Tiger Woods has already become a legendary **golfer**.   22. _____
23. The other poker players gave **Fred** encouragement to bet high.   23. _____
24. Their cheating made Fred the **loser** in the poker game.   24. _____
25. Fred, a trusting **fellow**, never caught on.   25. _____

In each sentence, fill in the blank with a noun of your own that **makes sense**. Then in the blank at the right, tell how that noun is **used** (use the abbreviations in parentheses):

subject (**subj**)   indirect object (**ind obj**)   appositive (**app**)
subjective complement (**subj comp**)   objective complement (**obj comp**)   direct address (**dir add**)
direct object (**dir obj**)   object of preposition (**obj prep**)

Example: We sang songs far into the <u>night</u>.   <u>obj prep</u>

(Collaborative option: Students work in pairs, alternating: one writes the word, the other names its use.)

1. First prize was a brand-new _____.   1. _____

2. _____, please make more coffee.   2. _____

3. The new _____ in town should expect a warm welcome.   3. _____

4. Every autumn the region's trees, mostly _____, delight touring leaf-peepers.   4. _____

5. Brad's CD collection contains mostly songs by _____.   5. _____

6. Before the examination Professor Ferrano gave us a(n) _____.   6. _____

7. Paula's attitude made her a(n) _____ to many classmates.   7. _____

8. Warmhearted Pat gave the _____ a hug.   8. _____

8. SENTENCES AND GRAMMAR: Complements

(Study 112B, Complements)

Part 1

In the blank, tell how each boldfaced complement is **used** (use the abbreviations in parentheses). If any complement is an adjective, **circle** it.

subjective complement (**subj comp**)   objective complement (**obj comp**)
direct object (**dir obj**)   indirect object (**ind obj**)

Examples: The ambassador delivered the **ultimatum**.   ___dir obj___
             The queen became (furious.)   ___subj comp___

1. The Lakers have been consistent **winners** in basketball.   1. _____
2. Sarah gave the **bedroom** a new coat of paint.   2. _____
3. The city lost many **jobs** after September 11, 2001.   3. _____
4. Kimiko declared English her **major**.   4. _____
5. The guide gave us **directions** to the Rue de la Paix.   5. _____
6. Friends, Romans, countrymen, lend **me** your ears.   6. _____
7. The soprano completed her **practice**.   7. _____
8. She sounds **happier** every day.   8. _____
9. **Whom** did you meet yesterday?   9. _____
10. Will the company give **John** another offer?   10. _____
11. Politicians will promise **us** anything.   11. _____
12. The group had been studying **anthropology** for three semesters.   12. _____
13. Her former employer gave **her** the idea for the small business.   13. _____
14. I named him my **beneficiary**.   14. _____
15. She is an **instructor** at the community college.   15. _____
16. She became an **administrator**.   16. _____
17. I found the **dictionary** under the bed.   17. _____
18. He considered her **brilliant**.   18. _____
19. Select whatever **medium** you like for your art project.   19. _____
20. The company made her **manager** of the branch office.   20. _____
21. Wasn't Eva's sculpture **stunning**?   21. _____
22. Please bake **me** an apple pie.   22. _____
23. Most women don't understand **menopause**.   23. _____
24. The toddler threw her **boots** against the wall.   24. _____
25. The besieging troops gave the surrounded city an **ultimatum** this morning.   25. _____

In each sentence, fill in the blank with a complement of your own. Then in the blank at the right, **tell what kind** of complement it is.

subjective complement (**subj comp**)   objective complement (**obj comp**)
direct object (**dir obj**)   indirect object (**ind obj**)

Example: The test results were <u>inconclusive</u>.   <u>subj comp</u>

(Collaborative option: Students work in pairs, alternating: one writes the word, the other names the kind of complement.)

1. This prescription drug is _____.   1. _____

2. The columnist received an anonymous _____.   2. _____

3. Santos named Ahmed his _____.   3. _____

4. Last year we did _____ a favor.   4. _____

5. The haunted house attracted curious _____ from far and near.   5. _____

6. This memo has caused _____ much grief.   6. _____

7. To be rid of him, they designated him _____.   7. _____

8. She did not seem particularly _____.   8. _____

9. SENTENCES AND GRAMMAR: Uses of Nouns

(Study 112, The Uses of Nouns)

First write a sentence of your own, using the boldfaced verb. Include the parts mentioned in parentheses (in the order given). Then **identify** each of those parts by writing its name under the proper word (use the abbreviations given below):

subject (**subj**)
subjective complement (**subj comp**)
direct object (**dir obj**)
indirect object (**ind obj**)

objective complement (**obj comp**)
object of preposition (**obj prep**)
appositive (**app**)
direct address (**dir add**)

Example: designated (subject, direct object, objective complement) <u>The teacher designated Paul the class librarian.</u>
                                        subj   dir obj   obj comp

(Collaborative option: Students work in pairs, alternating: one writes the sentence, the other identifies the uses.)

1. **destroyed** (Subject, direct object) _____

_____

2. **was** (Subject, subjective complement)_____

_____

3. **sent** (Subject, indirect object, direct object) _____

_____

4. **considered** (Subject, direct object, objective complement) _____

_____

_____

5. **sat** (Subject, appositive)_____

_____

6. **get** (Direct address, understood subject, direct object) _____

_____

7. **has obtained** (Subject, object of preposition, direct object)_____

_____

_____

8. **may show** (Subject, indirect object, direct object) _____

_____

9. **may become** (Subject, object of preposition, subjective complement) _____

_____

_____

10. **made** (Subject, direct object, objective complement)_____

_____

_____

11. **might have been** (Subject, appositive, subjective complement)_____

_____

_____

12. Make up your own verb. (Subject, direct object, appositive, objective complement)_____

_____

_____

_____

10. SENTENCES AND GRAMMAR: Verb Tenses and Forms

(Study 115, Principal Parts, and 116, Tense and Form)

Part 1

Identify the tense or other form of the boldfaced verb (use the abbreviations in parentheses):

present (**pres**)   past perfect (**past perf**)
past   future perfect (**fut perf**)
future (**fut**)   conditional (**cond**)
present perfect (**pres perf**)   past conditional (**past cond**)

Example: They **spoke** too fast for us.   ___past___

1. The operation **costs** $15,000.   1. _____
2. The plane **will** surely **depart** on time.   2. _____
3. Next summer, we **shall have lived** in this house for ten years. 3. _____
4. Billingsley Hall, our dormitory, **has acquired** a new coat of paint. 4. _____
5. By noon he **will have finished** the whole job.   5. _____
6. If the study were flawed, it **would be rejected**.   6. _____
7. **Shall** I ever **see** you again?   7. _____
8. Patriotic banners **appeared** all over town.   8. _____
9. At first they **had** not **believed** the rumors.   9. _____
10. If the study had been flawed, it **would have been rejected**.   10. _____
11. The company **guaranteed** that the package would arrive in the morning. 11. _____
12. Dylan **will begin** cello lessons in the spring.   12. _____
13. The children **have created** a snow castle in the front yard.   13. _____
14. **Have** you an extra set of car keys?   14. _____
15. They **would have passed** if they had studied harder.   15. _____
16. I **wrote** a review of the school play.   16. _____
17. The family **has planned** a vacation.   17. _____
18. The comic **laughed** at his own jokes.   18. _____
19. In one week the flu **hit** five staff members.   19. _____
20. This Friday **would have been** my grandmother's hundredth birthday. 20. _____
21. **Would** you **mind** if we left early?   21. _____
22. Congress **will have adjourned** by the time the law expires.   22. _____
23. Michael **has applied** for a junior year abroad.   23. _____
24. **Is** it fair for you to turn me down?   24. _____
25. Firefighters in the forest **braved** high winds and intense heat. 25. _____

In each blank, write the needed **ending**: **ed** (or **d**), **s** (or **es**), or **ing**. If no ending is needed, leave the blank empty.

Example: Every day the sun rise<u>s</u> later, and I wake_____ up later.

Today the brown cliffs rise_____ directly from the sea; no beach separate_____ the cliffs from the water. The waves have pound_____ the granite base of that cliff for ages but have fail_____ to wear it away. Now, as always, great white gulls are swoop_____ just above the foam; they are seek_____ fish that are destine_____ to become their dinner. Years ago, when my friend Jan and I first gather_____ the courage to approach the cliff's sheer edge and peer over, we imagine_____ what it would be like if we tumble_____ over and fell into that seething surf far below. At that time, the thought fill_____ me with terror.

Today, ten years later, as my friend and I stand_____ atop the cliffs, Jan speak_____ of how she felt then. I can tell that she is try_____ to relive that experience of our youth. We are not feel_____ the same terror now, and we will never feel_____ it again. Still, nothing would make_____ us go closer to the edge. When a man or woman reach_____ age thirty, he or she often attempt_____ to recapture the excitement of youth but rarely succeed_____. In a few moments Jan and I will walk_____ back to where our cars are park_____. We have been pretend_____ to be youngsters again, but now each of us know_____ that we can never repeat the past. Jan look_____ at me with a smile.

11. SENTENCES AND GRAMMAR: Verbs—Kind, Tense, Voice, and Mood

(Study 114, Kinds of Verbs; 115, Principal Parts; 116, Tenses, Forms; and 118, Avoiding Verb Errors)

Part 1

Write **T** if the verb is **transitive**.
Write **I** if it is **intransitive**.
Write **L** if it is **linking**.

Example: The house **looked** decrepit.	____L____
1. Jenny **kissed** me when we met.	1. _____
2. The thunder **sounded** louder each time.	2. _____
3. **Lay** your wet coat by the furnace.	3. _____
4. The roses **opened** early this spring.	4. _____
5. The island **lies** not far off the mainland.	5. _____
6. The last express **has** already **left**.	6. _____
7. **Set** the vase carefully on the table.	7. _____
8. Bosnik **remained** speaker of the Assembly for eight terms.	8. _____
9. Never **interfere** in another person's quarrel.	9. _____
10. The bus **departed** five minutes ago.	10. _____
11. Pollution **accumulated** in the atmosphere.	11. _____
12. The waiters **served** hors d'oeuvres before the main meal.	12. _____
13. My friend **seemed** nervous.	13. _____
14. The new class **ended** abruptly.	14. _____
15. Women **have been** instrumental in maintaining the social structure of the American Protestant churches.	15. _____

Part 2

Rewrite each boldfaced verb in the tense or form given in parentheses.

_____

Example: Now we **live** in Hamilton Hall. (present perfect)   _For the past year we have lived in Hamilton Hall._

1. Packing material from the box **clutters** the floor. (past)

_____

_____

2. The CIA **appointed** Choi its chief agent in Asia. (present perfect)

_____

_____

3. The CIA **appointed** Choi its chief agent in Asia. (past perfect)

_____

_____

4. The Red Sox **will win** the pennant by next fall. (future perfect)

_____

_____

5. The Everglades **will die** without relief from pollution. (conditional)

_____

_____

6. The Everglades **will die** without relief from pollution. (past conditional)

_____

_____

7. The Piffle Company **seeks** a new vice-president. (present progressive)

_____

_____

8. The Piffle Company **seeks** a new vice-president. (past emphatic)

_____

_____

9. The Piffle Company **seeks** a new vice-president. (present perfect)

_____

_____

10. The Piffle Company **seeks** a new vice-president. (present perfect progressive)

_____

_____

First write **A** if the boldfaced verb is in the **active voice** or **P** if it is in the **passive voice.** Then **rewrite** the sentence in the opposite voice (if it was active, make it passive; if it was passive, make it active). If necessary, supply your own subject.

Examples: A car **struck** the lamppost.   _____A_____
The lamppost was struck by a car.

The door **was left** open.   _____P_____
Someone left the door open.

1. One name **was** inadvertently **omitted** from the list.   1. _____

_____

_____

2. The negotiator **carried** a special agreement to the union meeting.   2. _____

_____

_____

3. The media **bashed** the incumbent's speech.   3. _____

_____

_____

4. The meeting **was called** to order.   4. _____

_____

_____

5. The ancient city **was** totally **destroyed** by a volcanic eruption.   5. _____

_____

_____

6. An accounting error **was discovered.**   6. _____

_____

_____

7. Younger voters **have selected** a presidential candidate.   7. _____

_____

_____

8. The prosecutor **subjected** the witness to a vigorous cross-examination.

8. _____

_____

_____

9. By dawn the police **will have barricaded** every road.

9. _____

_____

_____

10. The status report **will be submitted** next week.

10. _____

_____

_____

11. The left fielder **threw out** the runner.

11. _____

_____

_____

12. Environmental activists **have begun** a nationwide antipollution campaign.

12. _____

_____

_____

Part 4

Rewrite each sentence in the **subjunctive** mood.

Example: Today the sky is sunny.
        I wish the sky <u>were</u> sunny today.

1. Benito is on time.

   I wish Benito _____ on time.

2. I am a scuba diver; I search for sunken ships.

   If I _____ a scuba diver, I would search for sunken ships.

3. The customers insisted; their money was returned.

   The customers insisted that their money _____ returned.

12. SENTENCES AND GRAMMAR: Verbals

(Study 117, Distinguishing Verbals from Verbs)

Part 1

Identify each boldfaced verbal by writing
      inf for infinitive   **pres part** for present participle
      ger for gerund   **past part** for past participle

Example: The **outnumbered** soldiers surrendered.   **past part**

1. October is the best month **to watch** the falling leaves.   1._____

2. October is the best month to watch the **falling** leaves.   2._____

3. The next item on our agenda is **to select** a new secretary.   3._____

4. The next item on our agenda is **selecting** a new secretary.   4._____

5. I submitted a **typed** application.   5._____

6. **Encouraged** by their initial weight loss, Cecilia and Roy continued their diets.   6._____

7. **To lose** more weight, they had to both diet and exercise.   7._____

8. By **losing** weight, they felt and looked healthier.   8._____

9. **Ignoring** all criticism, Flo defended her friend's actions.   9._____

10. Flo likes **helping** her friends.   10._____

11. The movie *King Kong,* **seen** on a small TV screen, is much less impressive.   11._____

12. **Examining** the report, the consumer decided not to invest.   12._____

13. **Frightened,** he became cautious.   13._____

14. The purpose of the cookbook is **to reduce** the threat of cancer through a healthful diet.   14._____

15. **Reducing** carbon dioxide emissions was a top priority in a recent bill.   15._____

Complete each sentence with a verbal or verbal phrase of your own. Then in the blank at the right, tell how it is **used** (use the abbreviations in parentheses):

subject (**subj**)	object of preposition (**obj prep**)
subjective complement (**subj comp**)	adjective (**adj**)
direct object (**dir obj**)	adverb (**adv**)

Examples: <u>Faced with the evidence</u>, the suspect admitted the crime.   <u>adj</u>

The suspect was accused of <u>absconding with company funds</u>.   <u>obj prep</u>

(Collaborative option: Students work in pairs, alternating: one writes the word or phrase, the other identifies its use.)

1. _____ is no way to greet the day.   1. _____

2. Binoy likes _____.   2. _____

3. The _____ crowd rose to its feet.   3. _____

4. The driver got out and opened the hood [for what purpose?]

   _____   4. _____

5. Professor Zullo's obsession is _____

   _____   5. _____

6. I earned an *A* in her course by _____

   _____   6. _____

7. The huge motor home, _____

   _____, lumbered up the mountain road.   7. _____

8. As a last resort the officials tried _____

   _____   8. _____

9. My ambition since childhood has been _____

   _____   9. _____

10. Oddly, _____

   has never been one of my goals.   10. _____

13. SENTENCES AND GRAMMAR: Verbs

(Study 115, Principal Parts. 116, Tenses, Forms; and 118, Avoiding Verb Errors)

In each blank, write the **correct form** of the verb in parentheses (some answers may require more than one word).

Examples: (prefer) We have always <u>preferred</u> vanilla.
(see) Yesterday all of us <u>saw</u> the rainbow.

1. (use) The young man had never _____ a microwave.

2. (begin) He found the instruction book and _____ to read it.

3. (cross) They were _____ the busy street in the wrong place.

4. (blow) Trees of all sizes were _____ down in the storm.

5. (try) If I had found the courage, I would _____ _____ skydiving.

6. (drink) Drivers who had _____ alcoholic beverages were detained by the police.

7. (fly) By the time I reach Tokyo, I shall _____ _____ for thirteen hours nonstop.

8. (freeze) If they had not brought heavy clothing, they would _____ _____ on the hike.

9. (possess) The Tsar's court felt that Rasputin _____ a strange power over them.

10. (choose) The district has always _____ a Republican for Congress.

11. (bring) Sidney _____ his guitar to school last year.

12. (forbid) Yesterday the resident assistant _____ Sidney to play it after 9 p.m.

13. (lead) Firefighters _____ the children to safety when the smoke became too dense.

14. (lay) When their chores were finished, the weary farmers _____ their pitchforks against the fence and rested.

15. (pay) The company had always _____ its employees well.

16. (ring) The pizza deliverer walked up to the door and _____ the bell.

17. (rise) We are late; the sun has _____ already.

18. (see) Then I _____ him running around the corner.

19. (shine) Before the interview Rod _____ his old shoes.

20. (shine) Rod polished his car until it _____ brightly.

21. (break) The rebels had _____ the peace accord.

22. (shake) The medicine had to be _____ well before being used.

23. (struggle) For hours the fox had _____ _____ [2 words—use progressive form] to escape from the trap.

24. (show) Last week Ford _____ its new models at the automotive exhibition.

25. (mean) Daisy had not _____ to hit Mrs. Wilson.

26. (sink) In 1945 Nimitz's carrier planes _____ much of the enemy's fleet.

27. (drag) When it grew dark the poachers _____ the dead deer to their truck.

28. (speak) If they had known who she was, they never would _____ _____ to her.

29. (swing) In his last at-bat Pujols _____ the bat harder than ever before.

30. (throw) The pitcher had _____ a high fastball.

31. (write) A columnist had _____ that Pujols could not hit a high fastball.

32. (seek) After her divorce, Carla _____ a place of peace and quiet.

33. (admire) For years to come, people _____ _____ _____ [3 words—use progressive form] your paintings.

14. SENTENCES AND GRAMMAR: Using Verbs

(Study 115, Principal Parts, and 118, Avoiding Verb Errors)

Write **C** if the boldfaced verb is used **correctly**.
Write **X** if it is used **incorrectly**.

Examples: In chapter 1 Greg goes to war, and in chapter 10 he **died.** ____X____
The lake **was frozen** overnight by the sudden winter storm. ____C____

1. The longer he stayed, the more he **payed**. 1. _____

2. The pilots **have flown** this route hundreds of times. 2. _____

3. The giant shark **swam** far up the estuary. 3. _____

4. The phone **has rang** five times. Why don't you answer it? 4. _____

5. My hat **was stole** when I left it at the restaurant. 5. _____

6. We **have ridden** the train to Chicago many times. 6. _____

7. The little child **tore** open the present wrapped in bright yellow paper. 7. _____

8. The student **sunk** into his chair to avoid being called on by the professor. 8. _____

9. **Have** you **gone** to see the new *Star Wars* episode? 9. _____

10. We **should have known** that Robert would be late for the meeting. 10. _____

11. The little boy standing by the counter **seen** the man shoplift a watch. 11. _____

12. In the novel *Roscoe*, the main character decides to leave politics but **was drawn** back to it. 12. _____

13. The judge decreed that the abuser **be** sent to prison. 13. _____

14. The medals **shone** brightly on the general's uniform. 14. _____

15. The children **swang** on the swing until their mother called them home for supper. 15. _____

16. When we were small, we **wore** hats and white gloves on special occasions. 16. _____

17. The author **has**n't **spoken** to the news media for fifty years. 17. _____

18. Jack **wrote** his essay on the summer spent on his grandfather's farm. 18. _____

19. We **lay** on the couch reading the Sunday newspaper and munching doughnuts. 19. _____

20. Jack **stole** the chocolate candy when his brother left the kitchen. 20. _____

21. When Chillingworth realizes what Dimmesdale has been doing, he **began** to plot revenge. 21. _____

22. Only immigrants who could not afford first- or second-class ship fares **passed** through Ellis Island. 22. _____

23. Begin by taking Route 202 to West Chester; then you **should follow** Route 30 to Lancaster. 23. _____

24. Today long-distance telephone calls cost less than they **costed** forty years ago. 24. _____

25. Stella **has run** five miles along the coastal trail every day this year. 25. _____

26. Within ten minutes after someone broke into our house, the police **were notified** by us. 26. _____

27. The second act complicates the conflict, but the third act **resolves** it. 27. _____

28. Then I **come** up to him and said, "Let her alone!" 28. _____

29. McWilliams **has swum** from the mainland to Catalina Island. 29. _____

30. The pastor suggested that the discussion **be** postponed until the next Parish Council meeting. 30. _____

31. The child **was** finally **rescued** hours after falling into the pit. 31. _____

32. As the curtain rose, Bruce **is** standing alone on stage, peering out a window. 32. _____

33. The scientists' report **awakened** the nation to the dangers of overeating. 33. _____

15. SENTENCES AND GRAMMAR: Adjectives and Adverbs

(Study 119, Using Adjectives and Adverbs Correctly)

If the boldfaced adjective or adverb is used **correctly,** leave the blank empty.
If the boldfaced adjective or adverb is used **incorrectly,** write the correct word(s) in the blank.

Examples: Her performance was truly **impressive.**   _____
                 The Yankees are playing **good** this year.   _____well_____

1. The rock star sounds **good** on her new CD.   1._____
2. Why let his innocent remarks make you feel **badly**?   2._____
3. She was the **most** talented member of the dance couple.   3._____
4. Her computer is in very **good** condition for such an old machine. 4._____
5. He was very **frank** in his evaluation of his work.   5._____
6. My father spoke very **frankly** with us.   6._____
7. Her mother is the **kindest** of her two parents.   7._____
8. My stomach feels bad, and my back hurts **bad.**   8._____
9. The student looked **cheerful.**   9._____
10. The student looked **wearily** at the computer monitor.   10._____
11. I comb my hair **different** now.   11._____
12. Was the deer hurt **bad**?   12._____
13. He seemed **real** sad.   13._____
14. The learning assistant tried **awful** hard to keep the residence hall quiet during finals week. 14._____
15. Reading Eudora Welty's work is a **real** pleasure.   15._____
16. The teaching assistant glanced **nervously** at the class.   16._____
17. The bus driver seemed **nervous.**   17._____
18. The campus will look **differently** when the new buildings are completed. 18._____
19. Yours is the **clearest** of the two explanations.   19._____
20. The book is in **good** condition.   20._____
21. I did **poor** in organic chemistry this term.   21._____
22. Mario looked **debonair** in his new suit.   22._____
23. Trevor felt **badly** about having to fire the veteran employee. 23._____
24. Daryl's excuse was far **more poorer** than Keith's.   24._____
25. She writes very **well.**   25._____
26. It rained **steady** for the whole month of December in Houston. 26._____
27. The roses smell **sweet.**   27._____
28. He tries **hard** to please everyone.   28._____

29. John is **near** seven feet tall.   29._____

30. He talks **considerable** about his career plans.   30._____

31. She donated a **considerable** sum of money to the project.   31._____

32. The **smartest** of the twins is spoiled.   32._____

33. The **smartest** of the triplets is spoiled.   33._____

34. The coach gazed **uneasily** at her players.   34._____

35. He felt **uneasy** about the score.   35._____

36. Do try to drive more **careful**.   36._____

37. It was Bob's **most unique** idea ever.   37._____

38. The trial was **highly** publicized.   38._____

39. The wood carving on the left is even **more perfect** than the other one.   39._____

40. The house looked **strangely** to us.   40._____

41. She looked **strangely** at me, her brow furrowed.   41._____

42. He was ill, but he is **well** now.   42._____

43. That lobbyist is the most **influential** in Washington.   43._____

44. The orchestra sounded **good** throughout the hall.   44._____

45. Societal violence has **really** reached epidemic proportions in this country. 45._____

46. He seemed very **serious** about changing jobs.   46._____

47. Something in the refrigerator smelled **bad**.   47._____

48. We felt **badly** about missing the farewell party.   48._____

49. The police acted **swiftly** when they received the tip.   49._____

50. However, their response was not **swift** enough.   50._____

16. SENTENCES AND GRAMMAR: Articles and Determiners

(Study 120, Using Articles and Determiners Correctly)

Part 1

In each blank, write the **correct** article: **a, an,** or **the**; or leave the blank empty if **no** article is needed.
(In some blanks either of two answers is correct.)

Example: When the moon and a planet come close to each other in the sky, an exciting sight awaits _____ viewers.

_____ exciting play occurred yesterday in _____ big-league baseball game at _____ Dodger Stadium. _____ Dodger player dropped _____ ball in the glare of _____ sun. When _____ ball fell to _____ ground, three Dodger players ran after it; thus _____ nobody was guarding the bases for _____ Dodgers. _____ crowd groaned with _____ disappointment. _____ batter from _____ other team ran around _____ bases with _____ determination. _____ Dodger player retrieved _____ ball and made _____ accurate throw that reached home plate ahead of the runner, who was called "Out!" From the crowd came _____ cheers. The Dodgers won the game and celebrated with _____ champagne from _____ France. This was _____ biggest Dodger victory of the year.

Part 2

For each blank, choose from the list any correct determiner (limiting adjective), and write it in. Try not to use any word on the list more than once.

every	many	other	more	some
each	most	such	(a) little	
either	(a) few	both	much	
another	all	enough	any	

Example: They needed *another* person to help lift the car.

1. _____ country that voted for the United Nations resolution was praised.

2. _____ countries that voted against it were criticized.

3. _____ discussions took place before the vote.

4. _____ of the neutral countries tried to postpone the vote.

5. But _____ pressure was put on these countries to vote.

6. _____ effort to influence the neutral countries' vote was rebuffed.

7. Delegates from _____ countries wanted to get the voting finished.

8-9. _____ delegates had _____ patience.

10. Finally, the Secretary General declared that _____ voting would take place the next day.

17. SENTENCES AND GRAMMAR: Pronouns—Kind and Case

(Study 121, The Kinds of Pronouns, and 122, Using the Right Case)

Part 1

Classify each boldfaced pronoun (use the abbreviations in parentheses):

personal pronoun (**pers**)   indefinite pronoun (**indef**)
interrogative pronoun (**inter**)   reflexive pronoun (**ref**)
relative pronoun (**rel**)   intensive pronoun (**intens**)
demonstrative pronoun (**dem**)

Example: Who is your partner?   ___inter___

1. I made him an offer that **he** could not refuse.   1._____

2. I blame **no one** but myself for the error.   2._____

3. **This** is all I ask: that you tell me the truth.   3._____

4. I blame no one but **myself** for the error.   4._____

5. **Which** of the city newspapers do you read?   5._____

6. She is the executive **who** makes the key decisions in this company.   6._____

7. I **myself** have no desire to explore the rough terrain of mountainous regions.   7._____

8. **Everyone** promised to be on time for the staff meeting.   8._____

9. They chose three charities and gave a thousand dollars to each of **them.**   9._____

10. A small motor vehicle **that** can travel on rough woodland trails is called an all-terrain vehicle.   10._____

11. Be sure that you take care of **yourself** on the expedition.   11._____

12. These are my biology notes; **those** must be yours.   12._____

13. **Who** would you say is the most likely culprit?   13._____

14. If we lose, only we **ourselves** are to blame.   14._____

15. They requested that **neither** of the parties be informed.   15._____

Part 2

Write the number of the **correct** pronoun.

Example: The message was for Desmond and (1)**I** (2)**me**.   ___2___

1. None of (1)**we** (2)**us** plaintiffs felt that we had been adequately compensated.   1._____

2. Although I tried to be careful around the cat, I still stepped on (1)**its** (2)**it's** tail three times.   2._____

3. May we—John and (1)**I** (2)**me**—join you for the meeting?   3._____

4. Between you and (1)**I** (2)**me**, I feel quite uneasy about the outcome of the expedition.   4. _____

5. Were you surprised that the book was written by Jake and (1)**he** (2)**him**?   5. _____

6. It must have been (1)**he** (2)**him** who wrote the article about plant safety for the company newsletter.   6. _____

7. Why not support (1)**we** (2)**us** students in our efforts to have a new student union?   7. _____

8. No one except (1)**she** (2)**her** could figure out the copier machine.   8. _____

9. He is much more talented in dramatics than (1)**she** (2)**her**.   9. _____

10. The attorneys notified (1)**whoever** (2)**whomever** had a listed address.   10. _____

18. SENTENCES AND GRAMMAR: Pronouns—Case

(Study 122, Using the Right Case)

In the first blank, write the **number** of the **correct** pronoun.
In the second blank, write the **reason** for your choice (use the abbreviations in parentheses):

subject (**subj**)	indirect object (**ind obj**)
subjective complement (**subj comp**)	object of preposition (**obj prep**)
direct object (**dir obj**)	

Example: The tickets were for Jo and (1)**I** (2)**me**.   <u> 2 </u> <u>obj prep</u>

1. The queen knew that the traitor could be only (1)**he** (2)**him**.   1. ____ _____

2. Did you and (1)**he** (2)**him** ever find the tickets?   2. ____ _____

3. All of (1)**we** (2)**us** passengers were irked by the long delay at the airport.   3. ____ _____

4. Professor Fini showed (1)**they** (2)**them** the results of the experiment.   4. ____ _____

5. Sam Lewis preferred to be remembered as the person (1)**who** (2)**whom** invented the jalapeño-flavored lollipop.   5. ____ _____

6. I invited (1)**he** (2)**him** to the senior dance.   6. ____ _____

7. Speakers like (1)**she** (2)**her** are both entertaining and informative.   7. ____ _____

8. I was very much surprised when I saw (1)**he** (2)**him** at the art exhibit.   8. ____ _____

9. Have you and (1)**he** (2)**him** completed your research on the origins of American rodeos?   9. ____ _____

10. We asked Joan and (1)**he** (2)**him** about the playground activities.   10. ____ _____

11. The leader of the student group asked, "(1)**Who** (2)**Whom** do you think can afford the 10 percent increase in tuition?"   11. ____ _____

12. All of (1)**we** (2)**us** tourists spent the entire afternoon in a roadside museum.   12. ____ _____

13. It was (1)**he** (2)**him** who made all the arrangements for the dance.   13. ____ _____

14. Television network executives seem to think that ratings go to (1)**whoever** (2)**whomever** broadcasts the sexiest shows.   14. ____ _____

15. My two friends and (1)**I** (2)**me** decided to visit Window Rock, Arizona, headquarters of the Navajo nation.   15. ____ _____

16. This argument is just between Dick and (1)**I** (2)**me**.   16. ____ _____

17. My father always gave (1)**I** (2)**me** money for my tuition.   17. ____ _____

18. The cowboy movie star offered to co-produce a movie with (1)**whoever** (2)**whomever** promised an accurate portrayal of his life.   18. ____ _____

19. If you were (1)**I** (2)**me**, would you consider going on a summer cruise?   19. ____ _____

20. Gandhi, Mother Teresa, and Martin Luther King, Jr., are persons (1)**who** (2)**whom** I think will be remembered as heroes of the twentieth century.   20. ____ _____

21. Everyone was excused from class except Louise, Mary, and (1)**I** (2)**me**.   21. ____ _____

22. The teaching assistant asked (1)**he** (2)**him** about the experiment.   22. ____ _____

23. Nina was as interested as (1)**he** (2)**him** in moving to Florida after their retirement.   23. ____ _____

24. I knew of no one who had encountered more difficulties than (1)**she** (2)**her**.   24. ____ _____

25. Monisha gave (1)**I** (2)**me** the summary for our report.   25. ____ _____

26. The teachers invited (1)**we** (2)**us** parents to a meeting with an educational consultant.   26. ____ _____

27. The dance instructor was actually fifteen years older than (1)**he** (2)**him**.   27. ____ _____

28. (1)**We** (2)**Us** veterans agreed to raise money for a memorial plaque.   28. ____ _____

29. Are you and (1)**she** (2)**her** planning a joint report?   29. ____ _____

30. It is (1)**I** (2)**me** who am in charge of the bake sales for my children's school.   30. ____ _____

31. I am certain that he is as deserving of praise as (1)**she** (2)**her**.   31. ____ _____

32. If you were (1)**I** (2)**me**, where would you spend spring break?   32. ____ _____

33. (1)**Who** (2)**Whom** do you think will be the next mayor?   33. ____ _____

34. Assign the project to (1)**whoever** (2)**whomever** doesn't mind traveling.   34. ____ _____

35. She is a person (1)**who** (2)**whom** is, without question, destined to achieve success.   35. ____ _____

36. He is the author about (1)**who** (2)**whom** we shall be writing a paper.   36. ____ _____

37. Was it (1)**he** (2)**him** who won the contest?   37. ____ _____

38. The only choice left was between (1)**she** (2)**her** and him.   38. ____ _____

39. No one actually read the book except (1)**she** (2)**her**.   39. ____ _____

40. "Were you calling (1)**I** (2)**me**?" Jill asked as she entered the room.   40. ____ _____

41. Both of (1)**we** (2)**us** agreed that the exercise class was scheduled at an inconvenient time.   41. ____ _____

42. Imagine finally meeting (1)**he** (2)**him** after so many years of correspondence!   42. ____ _____

43. The poll takers asked both her friend and (1)**she** (2)**her** some very personal questions.   43. ____ _____

44. Do you suppose that (1)**he** (2)**him** will ever find time to come?   44. ____ _____

45. José sent an invitation to (1)**I** (2)**me**.   45. ____ _____

46. It was the other reviewer who disliked the movie, not (1)**I** (2)**me**.   46. ____ _____

47. The dean's objection to the content of our play caused the directors and (1)**we** (2)**us** much trouble.   47. ____ _____

48. A dispute arose about (1)**who** (2)**whom** would arrange the conference call.   48. ____ _____

49. Number 79 is the player (1)**who** (2)**whom** I believe scored the winning touchdown.   49. ____ _____

50. The flag will be raised by (1)**whoever** (2)**whomever** the mayor selects.   50. ____ _____

19. SENTENCES AND GRAMMAR: Pronoun Reference

(Study 123, Avoiding Faulty Reference)

Part 1

Write **C** if the boldfaced word is used **correctly**.
Write **X** if it is used **incorrectly**.

Example: Gulliver agreed with his master that **he** was a Yahoo.   ___X___

1. Dawna switched her major to physics; then she broke up with Rashid. None of us expected **this**.   1._____

2. Ms. Franco met Ms. Kazakovich at the jewelry counter when **she** was buying a necklace for her daughter.   2._____

3. The President later found his Middle East policy under attack by the opposing party. He resolved to ignore **that** criticism.   3._____

4. The latest of these attacks was so vicious that the Secretary of State urged the President to respond strongly to **it**.   4._____

5. The veteran football player practiced with the rookie because **he** wanted to review the new plays.   5._____

6. In Buffalo, **they** eat chicken wings served with blue cheese dressing and celery.   6._____

7. I was late filing my report, **which** greatly embarrassed me.   7._____

8. In the United States, **they** mail approximately 166 billion letters and packages each year.   8._____

9. She was able to complete college after earning a research assistantship. We greatly admire her for **that**.   9._____

10. The physician's speech focused on the country's inattention to the AIDS epidemic; the country was greatly surprised by **it**.   10._____

11. The President's dog was a favorite of the media, and **he** liked all that attention.   11._____

12. They intended to climb sheer Mount Maguffey; no one had ever accomplished **that** feat before.   12._____

13. Pat always wanted to be a television newscaster; thus she majored in **it** in college.   13._____

14. The average American child watches over thirty hours of television each week, **which** is why we are no longer a nation of readers.   14._____

15. **It** was well past midnight when the phone rang.   15._____

16. The speaker kept scratching his head, a mannerism **that** proved distracting.   16._____

17. According to the *Times,* **it** is expected to snow heavily in the upper Midwest this winter.   17._____

18. When Dan drives down the street in his red sports car, **they** all look on with admiration and, perhaps, just a little envy.   18._____

19. Aaron told Evan that **he** couldn't play in the soccer game.   19._____

20. Eric started taking pictures in high school. **This** interest led to a brilliant career in photography.   20._____

21. **It** is best to be aware of both the caloric and fat content of food in your diet.   21._____

22. In some vacation spots, **they** add the tip to the bill and give poor service.   22._____

23. In Russo's novel *Empire Falls*, the main character seems just like **him**.   23. _____

24. In some sections of the country **it** seemed as if the drought would never end.   24. _____

25. In some sections of the history text, it seems as if **they** ignored women's contributions to the development of this country.   25. _____

Choose eight items that you marked **X** in part 1. **Rewrite** each correctly in the blanks below. Before each sentence, write its number from part 1.

Example: 26. *Gulliver agreed that he was a Yahoo, as his master said.*

_____

_____

_____

_____

_____

_____

_____

_____

_____

_____

_____

_____

_____

_____

_____

_____

20. SENTENCES AND GRAMMAR: Phrases

(Study 124, Phrases)

Part 1

In the first blank, write the number of the **one** set of words that is a prepositional phrase.
In the second blank, write **adj** if the phrase is used as an adjective, or **adv** if it is used as an adverb.

Example: <u>The starting pitcher</u> <u>for the Giants</u> <u>is a left-hander.</u>   <u> 2 </u> <u>adj</u>
               1   2   3

1. <u>If time permits,</u> <u>the club members</u> <u>will vote today</u> <u>on your proposal</u>.   1. ____ ____
      1   2   3   4

2. <u>The great white pines</u> <u>growing in the northern forests</u> <u>may soon die</u> <u>without more rain</u>.   2. ____ ____
        1   2   3   4

3. <u>The lady</u> <u>wearing the fur stole</u> <u>has been dating</u> <u>an animal activist</u> <u>from Oregon</u>.   3. ____ ____
      1   2   3   4   5

4. <u>What they saw</u> <u>before the door closed</u> <u>shocked them</u> <u>beyond belief</u>.   4. ____ ____
       1   2   3   4

5. <u>The most frequently used word</u> <u>in the English language</u> <u>is the word</u> *the*.   5. ____ ____
           1   2   3

6. <u>The need</u> <u>for adequate child care</u> <u>was not considered</u> <u>when the President addressed the convention</u>.   6. ____ ____
      1   2   3   4

7. <u>The observation</u> <u>that men and women have different courtship rituals</u> <u>seems debatable</u>
      1   2   3

     <u>in a modern postindustrial society</u>.   7. ____ ____
           4

8. <u>At our yard sale,</u> <u>I found out</u> <u>that people will buy almost anything</u> <u>if the price is right</u>.   8. ____ ____
        1   2   3

9. <u>Until the last five minutes</u> <u>our team seemed</u> <u>to have the game won,</u> <u>but we lost</u>.   9. ____ ____
           1   2   3   4

10. <u>After everyone left</u> <u>to attend the meeting,</u> <u>Nugent sneaked back</u> <u>for a long, quiet nap</u>.   10. ____ ____
        1   2   3   4

Some of the boldfaced expressions are verbal phrases; others are parts of verbs (followed by modifiers or complements). In the blank, **identify** each **expression** (use the abbreviations in parentheses):

verbal phrase used as adjective (**adj**)
verbal phrase used as adverb (**adv**)
verbal phrase used as noun (**noun**)
part of verb (with modifiers or complements) (**verb**)

Examples: Singing in the rain can give one a cold.   <u> noun </u>
             Gene is **singing in the rain** despite his cold.   <u> verb </u>

1. **Speaking from the Capitol steps** is a favorite act of politicians.   1. _____

2. Senator Claghorn is **speaking from the Capitol steps** today.   2. _____

3. **To prepare his income taxes,** Sam spent several hours sorting through the shoe boxes filled with receipts.   3. _____

4. By age 30, many women begin **sensing a natural maternal need.**   4. _____

5. Both lawyers, **having presented their closing arguments**, nervously awaited the jury's verdict.   5. _____

6. The Clementes were **having the Robertsons to dinner that evening**.   6. _____

7. His idea of a thrill is **driving in stock-car races.**   7. _____

8. **Driving in stock-car races**, he not only gets his thrills but also earns prize money.   8. _____

9. Her congregation is **surviving on a very small income**.   9. _____

10. She earnestly desires **to increase the membership**.   10. _____

21. SENTENCES AND GRAMMAR: Verbal Phrases

(Study 124B, The Verbal Phrase)

Part 1

In each sentence, find a verbal phrase. **Circle** it, and in the small blank at the right, tell how it is used: as adjective (write **adj**), adverb (write **adv**), or **noun**.

Example: A study (conducted by the Yale Medical School) found that smoking is addictive.   _____adj_____

1. Holding the flag high, the veterans marched down Main Street.   1. _____

2. Leading the Memorial Day parade was an honored tradition for the veterans.   2. _____

3. Topic selection is the first step in producing a research paper.   3. _____

4. Hopelessly in love, June neglected to go to her science class.   4. _____

5. The Secretary of State, realizing the need for negotiation, arranged a peace conference between the belligerents.   5. _____

6. To provide safe neighborhoods, the police have begun intensified nighttime patrols.   6. _____

7. I can't help liking her even though she isn't interested in my favorite sport, hockey.   7. _____

8. Disappointed with her grades, Sabrina made an appointment with her counselor.   8. _____

9. I appreciate your helping us at the craft fair.   9. _____

10. Our lacrosse team, beaten in the playoffs, congratulated the winners.   10. _____

11. They changed all the locks to feel more safe.   11. _____

12. No matter how often the teacher told them to be quiet, the kindergartners chattered and fidgeted constantly.   12. _____

13. Rock climbing is a sport demanding endurance.   13. _____

14. I passed chemistry by studying past midnight all last week.   14. _____

15. The hunter put down his gun, realizing that the ducks had flown out of range.   15. _____

Part 2

Complete each sentence with a verbal phrase of your own. Then, in the small blank at the right, tell how you used it: **adj**, **adv**, or **noun**.

1. To take the test without _____ was not wise at all.   1. _____

2. Alison organized a group of senior citizens [hint: for what purpose?] _____   2. _____
   _____.

3. Worried about her children, the young mother decided _____   3. _____
   _____.

4. _____ may be

   linked to increased risk of rectal and bladder cancer.   4. _____

5. She tried to obtain the information without _____

   _____.   5. _____

6. The student _____ is here to

   select a major.   6. _____

7. The best book _____ is one

   that helps you escape daily tension.   7. _____

8. _____, he found an article

   that was easy to understand.   8. _____

9. Physicians recommend that patients _____

   donate their own blood.   9. _____

10. _____ has been

    the cause of too many fires.   10. _____

22. SENTENCES AND GRAMMAR: Review of Phrases

(Study 124, Phrases; also suggested: 128E, Use Reduction)

Part 1

Classify each boldfaced phrase (use the abbreviations in parentheses):

prepositional phrase (**prep**)   gerund phrase (**ger**)

infinitive phrase (**inf**)   absolute phrase (**abs**)

participial phrase (**part**)

Example: The economies **of Asian countries** grew shaky.   _____prep_____

1. The reddish bird flitting **among the weeds** is a rufous-sided towhee.   1. _____
2. The reddish bird **flitting among the weeds** is a rufous-sided towhee.   2. _____
3. The first televisions had small round screens encased **in large wooden cabinets.**   3. _____
4. **His insisting that he was right** made him unpopular with his associates.   4. _____
5. The committee voted **to adjourn immediately.**   5. _____
6. **Because of the storm**, the excursion around the lake had to be postponed.   6. _____
7. **To stay awake in Smedley's class** required dedication and plenty of black coffee.   7. _____
8. **During early television programming**, many commercials were five minutes long.   8. _____
9. **Flying a jet at supersonic speeds** has been Sally's dream since childhood.   9. _____
10. We were obliged to abandon our plans, **the boat having been damaged in a recent storm.**   10. _____
11. **Realizing that his back injury would get worse**, the star player retired from professional basketball.   11. _____
12. **To pay for their dream vacation**, Harry and Sue both took on extra jobs.   12. _____
13. The children were successful in **developing their own lawn-mowing company.**   13. _____
14. **The semester completed**, students were packing up to go home.   14. _____
15. The distinguished-looking man **in the blue suit** is the head of the company.   15. _____
16. **Earning a college degree** used to guarantee a well-paying job.   16. _____
17. Approximately one-fourth **of the American work force** has a college degree.   17. _____
18. On May 11, 1939, the first baseball game was telecast **in America.**   18. _____
19. Deciding which car **to buy** is a difficult task.   19. _____
20. Two crates **of oranges** were delivered to the fraternity house.   20. _____
21. **Anticipating an overflow audience**, the custodian put extra chairs in the auditorium.   21. _____
22. A car **filled with students** left early this morning to arrange for the class picnic.   22. _____
23. The agent **wearing an official badge** is the one to see about tickets.   23. _____
24. **Her mind going blank at the last minute,** Madeline could not answer the quizmaster's million-dollar question.   24. _____

25. **Frequently checking one's bank-account balance** can prevent embarrassing "insufficient funds" check returns.

25. _____

Part 2

Combine the following pairs of sentences by reducing one of the sentences to a phrase.

Examples: The new furniture arrived yesterday. It was for the den.
The new furniture for the den arrived yesterday.

Professor Hughes gave us an assignment. We had to find five library references on the Depression.
Professor Hughes gave us an assignment to find five library references on the Depression.

(Collaborative option: Students work in pairs or small groups to suggest ways of combining.)

1. Fred flipped through the channels. He decided that reading the phone book would be more exciting than watching television.

_____

_____

_____

2. Scientists are using artificial life simulation programs. They are doing this for futuristic experimentation.

_____

_____

_____

3. North America, Asia, and Europe must work together. That way they can prevent the holes in the ozone layer from becoming any larger.

_____

_____

_____

4. The international community has responded to the September 11, 2001, attacks. It has revamped its undercover operations.

_____

_____

_____

5. In the 1920s Americans often used homemade crystal radio sets. They did this so that they could listen to radio broadcasts.

_____

_____

_____

6. His weekend was ruined. So Alfredo decided to go to bed early.

_____

_____

_____

7. The white potato plant was grown strictly as an ornament in Europe. This was before the 1700s.

_____

_____

_____

8. American widows report that friends and relatives interfere too much. These widows frequently prefer to spend time alone.

_____

_____

_____

23. SENTENCES AND GRAMMAR: Recognizing Clauses

(Study 125, Clauses)

Classify each boldfaced clause (use the abbreviations in parentheses):

independent [main] clause (**ind**)
dependent [subordinate] clause: adjective clause (**adj**)
adverb clause (**adv**)
noun clause (**noun**)

Example: The program will work **when the disk is inserted**.   ___adv___

1. The house had a long flight of steps leading to the first floor **because it was built on the side of a hill**.   1. _____

2. Farmers asked the government for disaster relief because of the drought, **which had by then lasted nearly four years**.   2. _____

3. The tourists asked **how they could reach Times Square by subway**.   3. _____

4. The student **who made the top grade in the history quiz** is my roommate.   4. _____

5. **Whether I am able to go to college** depends on whether I can find employment. 5. _____

6. **After Judd had written a paper for his English class**, he watched television. 6. _____

7. Canada celebrates Thanksgiving in October; **the United States celebrates it in November**. 7. _____

8. The career center offers seminars to anyone **who needs help writing a résumé**. 8. _____

9. There is much excitement **whenever election results are announced**.   9. _____

10. The detective listened carefully to the suspect's answers, but **she couldn't find a reason to charge the suspect**.   10. _____

11. Few Americans realize **that their homes are full of minute dust mites**.   11. _____

12. My first impression was **that someone had been in my room quite recently**.   12. _____

13. The actor **who had lost the Oscar** declared through clenched teeth that she was delighted just to have been nominated.   13. _____

14. He dropped a letter in the mailbox; **then he went to the library**.   14. _____

15. The candidate decided to withdraw from the city council race **because she didn't approve of the media's treatment of her mental illness**.   15. _____

16. Why don't you sit here **until the rest of the class arrives**?   16. _____

17. The real estate mogul, **who is not known for his modesty**, has named still another building after himself.   17. _____

18. **Although he is fifty-two years old**, he is very youthful in appearance.   18. _____

19. The Battle of Saratoga is more famous, yet **the Battle of Brandywine involved more soldiers**. 19. _____

20. **Why she never smiles** is a mystery to her colleagues.   20. _____

21. **Why don't you wait** until you have all the facts?   21. _____

22. She is a person **whom everyone respects and admires**.   22. _____

23. The weather is surprisingly warm **even though it is December**.   23. _____

24. My answer was **that I had been unavoidably detained**.   24. _____

25. The cat loved to sleep in the boys' room **because it could stalk their goldfish at night.**   25. _____

26. The trophy will be awarded to **whoever wins the contest.**   26. _____

27. The detective walked up the stairs; **she opened the door of the guest room.**   27. _____

28. Is this the book **that you asked us to order for you**?   28. _____

29. The audience could not believe **that the show would be delayed for an hour**.   29. _____

30. My Aunt Minnie Matilda, **who wrote piano duets for children**, died penniless.   30. _____

31. **Because students are prone to resolving conflicts by fighting with one another**, the principal is working on developing conflict resolution groups.   31. _____

32. The log cabin **where my father was born** is still standing.   32. _____

33. Many Americans realize **that dual-income families are a result of a declining economy rather than gender equality.**   33. _____

24. SENTENCES AND GRAMMAR: Dependent Clauses

(Study 125B, Kinds of Dependent Clauses; also suggested: 128D, Use Subordination)

Part 1

Underline the dependent clause in each item. Then, in the blank, **classify** it as an adjective (**adj**), adverb (**adv**), or **noun**.

Example: The textbook explained fully <u>what the instructor had outlined</u>.   <u> noun </u>

1. Although he was an experienced tree-cutter, his miscalculation brought the giant oak down on the garage roof.   1._____

2. The couple searched the Internet for a vacation spot where cell phones could not reach them.   2._____

3. The early bicycles weren't comfortable, because they had wooden wheels and wooden seats.   3._____

4. The student who complained about the food was given another dessert.   4._____

5. Whether Camille dyes her hair remains a mystery.   5._____

6. After Jonathan had read the morning paper, he threw up his hands in despair.   6._____

7. Whoever predicted today's widespread use of computers was truly a prophet.   7._____

8. Professor George gave extra help to anyone who asked for it.   8._____

9. There is always much anxiety whenever final exams are held.   9._____

10. Studies show that calcium intake among American teenagers is often inadequate.   10._____

Part 2

In each long blank, write a dependent clause of your own. Then, in the small blank, **identify** your clause as adjective (**adj**), adverb (**adv**), or **noun**.

Example: The noted author, <u>who was autographing her books</u>, smiled at us.   <u> adj </u>

(Collaborative option: Students work in pairs, alternating: one writes the clause, the other tells how it is used.)

1. Dr. Jackson,_____,
   declared Burton the winner.   1._____

2. The award went to the actor _____.   2._____

3. _____,
   parents are spending less time with their children.   3._____

4. Luis remarked _____.   4._____

5. _____,
   Congress voted against the bill.   5._____

6. It was the only mistake _____.   6._____

7. During his presentation, Nathan explained _____

   _____.   7._____

8. Most of the audience had tears in their eyes _____

   _____ .   8. _____

9. The United States, _____ ,

   is still the preferred destination of millions of immigrants.   9. _____

10. The candidate told her followers _____ .   10. _____

25. SENTENCES AND GRAMMAR: Noun and Adjective Clauses

(Study 125B, Kinds of Dependent Clauses; also suggested: 128D, Use Subordination)

Combine each of the following pairs of sentences into one sentence. Do this by reducing one of the pair to a noun or adjective clause.

Examples: Something puzzled the police. What did the note mean?
<u>What the note meant puzzled the police.</u>
The X-Files became immensely popular in the late 1990s. It appeared on the Fox TV network.
<u>The X-Files, which appeared on the Fox TV network, became immensely popular in the late 1990s.</u>

(Collaborative option: Students work in pairs or small groups to suggest ways of combining.)

1. One thing remained unresolved. Who was the more accomplished chef? [Hint: try a noun clause.]

   _____

   _____

2. The programmer retired at age twenty. She had written the new computer game. [Hint: try an adjective clause.]

   _____

   _____

3. I do not see how anyone could object to that. The senator said it.

   _____

   _____

4. The laboratory assistant gave the disk to Janine. He had helped Janine learn the word-processing software.

   _____

   _____

5. They planned something for the scavenger hunt. It seemed really bizarre.

   _____

   _____

6. We should spend the money on someone. Who needs it most?

   _____

   _____

7. Large classes and teacher apathy are problems. Most school districts tend to ignore them.

    _____

    _____

8. Every teacher has a worst fear. Her students may hate to read.

    _____

    _____

9. Glenn was a certain kind of person. He seemed to thrive on hard work and tight deadlines.

    _____

    _____

10. Animal rights activists demonstrated in certain states. In these states grizzly bear hunting is allowed.

    _____

    _____

11. Samuel F. B. Morse is famous for pioneering the telegraph. He was also a successful portrait painter.

    _____

    _____

12. Something could no longer be denied. The war was already lost.

    _____

    _____

13. The long black limousine had been waiting in front of the building. It sped away suddenly.

    _____

    _____

14. When Columbus reached America, there were more than three hundred Native American tribes. Together these tribes contained more than a million people.

    _____

    _____

15. You must decide something now. That thing is critically important.

    _____

    _____

16. My English professor has written a biography of Bret Harte. She is obviously enthralled by this nineteenth-century writer.

    _____

    _____

17. The jackpot will be won by someone. That person holds the lucky number.

    _____

    _____

18. Juan has a friendly disposition. It has helped him during tense negotiations at work.

    _____

    _____

19. The TV news reported things regarding the episode. We were appalled by them.

    _____

    _____

20. Paleontologists have unearthed a set of bones. They make up the most nearly complete Tyrannosaurus Rex ever found.

    _____

    _____

    _____

26. SENTENCES AND GRAMMAR: Adverb Clauses

(Study 125B, Kinds of Dependent Causes; also suggested: 128D, Use Subordination)

Combine each of the following pairs of sentences into one sentence by reducing one sentence to the kind of adverb clause specified in brackets.

Examples: The sun set. Then the lovers headed home. [time]
　　　　　　When the sun set, the lovers headed home.
　　　　　Students must score 1400 on their College Boards. Otherwise they will not be admitted. [condition]
　　　　　Students will not be admitted unless they score 1400 on their College Boards.

(Collaborative option: Students work in pairs or small groups to suggest ways of combining.)

1. [cause] Four hundred thousand Americans each year get skin cancer. Therefore, many parents are teaching their children to avoid overexposure to sunlight.

　　_____

　　_____

　　_____

2. [place] The candidate was willing to speak anywhere. But she had to find an audience there.

　　_____

　　_____

3. [manner] Carl ran the race. He seemed to think his life depended on it.

　　_____

　　_____

4. [comparison] Her brother has always been able to read fast. She has always been able to read faster.

　　_____

　　_____

5. [purpose] This species of tree has poisonous leaves. That way, insects will not destroy it.

　　_____

　　_____

6. [time] The concert was half over. Most of the audience had already left.

　　_____

　　_____

7. [comparison] I worked hard on that project. I could not have worked harder.

_____

_____

8. [purpose] He read extensively. His purpose was to be well prepared for the test.

_____

_____

9. [condition] American attitudes must change. Otherwise small family farms will disappear.

_____

_____

10. [concession] Her grades were satisfactory. But she did not qualify for the scholarship.

_____

_____

11. [result] She worried very much. The result was that she could no longer function effectively.

_____

_____

12. [condition] You may accept the position, or you may not. Either way, you should write a thank-you note to the interviewer.

_____

_____

13. [cause] Frosts destroyed Florida's citrus crops this year. So citrus prices will increase significantly.

_____

_____

14. [condition] Do not complete the rest of the form yet. You have to see your advisor first.

_____

_____

15. [concession] Marina was only 5 feet 5 inches tall. But she was determined to be a basketball star.

_____

_____

16. [place] Fahnestock preferred one kind of vacation place. No one stood in line for anything there.

_____

_____

17. [condition] The substance may be an acid. Then the litmus paper will turn red.

_____

_____

18. [cause] Ethnic jokes can be particularly harmful. Such humor subtly reinforces stereotypes.

_____

_____

19. [manner] She smiled in a certain way. Maybe she knew something unsuspected by the rest of us.

_____

_____

20. [comparison] Horgan received good grades. But Schultz usually received better ones.

_____

_____

27. SENTENCES AND GRAMMAR: Kinds of Sentences

(Study 125C, Clauses in Sentences; also suggested: 128B–E, Use Coordination, Compounding, Subordination, and Reduction)

Part 1

Classify each sentence (use the abbreviations in parentheses):

simple (**sim**)   complex (**cx**)
compound (**cd**)   compound-complex (**cdcx**)

Example: Hank opened the throttle, and the boat sped off.   _____cd_____

1. The governor maintained that the state's finances were sound.   1. _____

2. Ted Williams, whose .406 season batting average has been unequaled for more than sixty years, had amazingly sharp eyes.   2. _____

3. Completion of the new library will be delayed unless funds become available.   3. _____

4. Consider the matter carefully before you decide; your decision will be final.   4. _____

5. This year, either medical companies or discount store chains are a good investment for the small investor.   5. _____

6. The play, which was written and produced by a colleague, was well received by the audience.   6. _____

7. The storm, which had caused much damage, subsided; we then continued on our hike.   7. _____

8. We waited until all the spectators had left the gymnasium.   8. _____

9. The argument having been settled, the meeting proceeded more or less amicably.   9. _____

10. The prescription was supposed to cure my hives; instead it made my condition worse.   10. _____

11. Tired of being a spy, he settled in Vermont and began writing his memoirs.   11. _____

12. His chief worry was that he might reveal the secret by talking in his sleep.   12. _____

13. The television special accurately portrayed life in the 1950s; critics, therefore, praised the production for its authenticity.   13. _____

14. The story appearing in the school paper contained several inaccuracies.   14. _____

15. The police officer picked up the package and inspected it carefully.   15. _____

16. Because she was eager to get an early start, Sue packed the night before.   16. _____

17. By 2080, there will be over one million Americans one hudred years old or older; this significant increase of centenarians will profoundly affect the health care system.   17. _____

18. Noticing the late arrivals, the speaker motioned for them to be seated.   18. _____

19. A study of people in their eighties revealed that most had a satisfying relationship with a family member or care provider; in other words, these older Americans were not lonely in their old age.   19. _____

20. Through the thick fog rolling in from the sea, Courtney could barely discern the tail lights of a car farther along the beach.   20. _____

In the long blank, **combine** each set of sentences into one sentence. Then, in the small blank, **classify** your new sentence as simple (**sim**), compound (**cd**), complex (**cx**), or compound-complex (**cdcx**).

Examples: The President flew to Gibraltar. From there she cruised to Malta.
The President flew to Gibraltar and from there cruised to Malta.   ____sim____

    The ballerina's choreography won praise that night. She was not satisfied with it.
        She spent the next morning reworking it.
Although the ballerina's choreography won praise that night, she was not satisfied
with it and spent the next morning reworking it.   ____cx____

(Collaborative option: Students work in pairs or small groups to suggest ways of combining.)

1. The suspect went to the police station. She turned herself in.

    1. _____

2. The little girl won the poetry contest. She plans to be a writer.

    2. _____

3. We wanted that house. It was already sold. So we had to look for another one.

    3. _____

4. Batik is a distinctive and complex method of dyeing cloth. It was created on the island of Java.

    4. _____

5. Scientists convened. They came from all over the world. They wanted to discuss the greenhouse effect. This was a serious problem.

    5. _____

6. In the 1920s there were three favorite amusements. They were mahjong, ouija, and crossword puzzles.

6. _____

7. Only one country has a lower personal income tax than the United States. That is Japan. This is among the wealthy nations.

7. _____

8. The American Dream seems inaccessible to many Americans. These Americans have difficulty even making ends meet.

8. _____

9. Some couples marry before age thirty. These couples have a high divorce rate.

9. _____

10. Banks make this promise to their customers. Banking will become more convenient. It will happen through computer technology.

10. _____

11. Erskine smacked his lips. He plowed through another stack of buttermilk pancakes. They were smothered in blueberry syrup.

11. _____

12. The Middle East is the birthplace of three major world religions. One is Judaism. Another is Christianity. The third is Islam.

12. _____

13. The women sat up talking. They did this late one night. They talked about their first dates. Most laughed about their teenage years. These years had been awkward.

13. _____

_____

_____

_____

28. SENTENCES AND GRAMMAR: Subject-Verb Agreement

(Study 126, Subject-Verb Agreement)

Write the number of the **correct** choice.

Example: One of the network's best programs (1)**was** (2)**were** canceled. _____1_____

1. Neither the men's nor the women's room (1)**has** (2)**have** been cleaned today. 1._____

2. Physics (1)**is** (2)**are** among the hardest majors in the curriculum. 2._____

3. Working a second job to pay off my debts (1)**has** (2)**have** become a priority. 3._____

4. Not one of the nominees (1)**has** (2)**have** impressed me. 4._____

5. (1)**Does** (2)**Do** each of the questions count the same number of points? 5._____

6. The number of jobs lost in California's Silicon Valley (1)**has** (2)**have** increased significantly in the past two years. 6._____

7. *Ninety-nine* (1)**is** (2)**are** hyphenated because it is a compound number. 7._____

8. The college president, along with five vice-presidents, (1)**was** (2)**were** ready for the meeting. 8._____

9. Both the secretary and the treasurer (1)**was** (2)**were** asked to submit reports. 9._____

10. Everyone in the audience (1)**was** (2)**were** surprised by the mayor's remarks. 10._____

11. *Women* (1)**is** (2)**are** spelled with an *o* but pronounced with an *i* sound. 11._____

12. Every junior and senior (1)**was** (2)**were** expected to report to the gymnasium. 12._____

13. There (1)**is** (2)**are** a professor, several students, and a teaching assistant meeting to discuss the course reading list. 13._____

14. Ten dollars (1)**is** (2)**are** too much to pay for that book. 14._____

15. (1)**Is** (2)**Are** there any computers available in the lab this morning? 15._____

16. Neither the neighbors nor the police officer (1)**was** (2)**were** surprised by the violent crime. 16._____

17. Each of the crises actually (1)**needs** (2)**need** the President's immediate attention. 17._____

18. (1)**Is** (2)**Are** your father and brother coming to see you graduate tomorrow? 18._____

19. A good book and some chocolate doughnuts (1)**was** (2)**were** all she needed to relax. 19._____

20. There (1)**is** (2)**are** one coat and two hats in the hallway. 20._____

21. (1)**Does** (2)**Do** Coach Jasek and the players know about the special award? 21._____

22. My two weeks' vacation (1)**was** (2)**were** filled with many projects around the house. 22._____

23. The only thing that annoyed me more (1)**was** (2)**were** the children's tracking mud in from the backyard. 23._____

24. (1)**Hasn't** (2)**Haven't** either of the roommates looked for the missing ring? 24._____

25. There (1)**is** (2)**are** a bird and a squirrel fighting over the birdseed in the feeder. 25._____

26. On the table (1)**was** (2)**were** a pen, a pad of paper, and two rulers. 26._____

27. It is remarkable that the entire class (1)**is** (2)**are** taking the field trip. 27._____

28. It (1)**was** (2)**were** a book and a disk that disappeared from the desk. 28._____

29. There (1)**is** (2)**are** many opportunities for part-time employment on campus.   29. _____

30. (1)**Is** (2)**Are** algebra and chemistry required courses?   30. _____

31. One of his three instructors (1)**has** (2)**have** offered to write a letter of recommendation.   31. _____

32. (1)**Does** (2)**Do** either of the books have a section on usage rules?   32. _____

33. Neither my parents' car nor our own old Jeep (1)**is** (2)**are** reliable enough to make the trip.   33. _____

34. Marbles, stones, and string (1)**is** (2)**are** my son's favorite playthings.   34. _____

35. Each of the books (1)**has** (2)**have** an introduction written by the author's mentor.   35. _____

36. The lab report, in addition to several short papers, (1)**was** (2)**were** due immediately after spring break.   36. _____

37. Neither the teacher nor the parents (1)**understands** (2)**understand** why Nathan does so well in math but can barely read first-grade books.   37. _____

38. The old woman who walks the twin Scottish terriers (1)**detests** (2)**detest** small children running on the sidewalk in front of her house.   38. _____

39. At the Boy Scout camp-out, eggs and bacon (1)**was** (2)**were** the first meal the troop attempted to prepare on an open fire.   39. _____

40. (1)**There's** (2)**There are** more butter and mayonnaise in the refrigerator.   40. _____

41. Everyone (1)**was** (2)**were** working hard to finish planting the crops before the rainy season.   41. _____

42. The children, along with their teacher, (1)**is** (2)**are** preparing a one-act play for the spring open house.   42. _____

43. Minnie Olson is one of those people who always (1)**volunteers** (2)**volunteer** to help the homeless.   43. _____

44. Lucy announced that *The Holy Terrors* (1)**is** (2)**are** the title of her next book, which is about raising her three sons.   44. _____

45. The class, along with the teacher, (1)**was** (2)**were** worried about the ailing class pet.   45. _____

46. Five dollars (1)**does** (2)**do** not seem like much to my eight-year-old son.   46. _____

47. Either the choir members or the organist (1)**was** (2)**were** constantly battling with the minister about purchasing fancy new choir robes.   47. _____

48. In the last 200 years, over 50 million people from 140 countries (1)**has** (2)**have** left their homelands to immigrate to the United States.   48. _____

49. Food from different geographic locations and ethnic groups often (1)**helps** (2)**help** distinguish specific cultural events.   49. _____

50. Virtually every painting and every sculpture Picasso did (1)**is** (2)**are** worth over a million dollars.   50. _____

51. There on the table (1)**was** (2)**were** my wallet and my key chain.   51. _____

52. Neither the documentary about beekeeping nor the two shows about Iceland (1)**was** (2)**were** successful in the ratings.   52. _____

53. Each of the new television series (1)**is** (2)**are** about single-parent families.   53. _____

54. Sitting on the sidewalk (1)**was** (2)**were** Amy and her four best friends.   54. _____

55. *Les Atrides* (1)**is** (2)**are** a ten-hour, four-play production of ancient Greek theater.   55. _____

56. A political convention, with its candidates, delegates, and reporters, (1)**seems** (2)**seem** like bedlam.   56. _____

57. In the auditorium (1)**was** (2)**were** assembled the orchestra members who were ready to practice for the upcoming concert.

57. _____

58. Each of the art historians (1)**has** (2)**have** offered a theory for why the Leonardo painting has such a stark background.

58. _____

59. (1)**Was** (2)**Were** either President Smith or Dean Nicholson asked to speak at the awards ceremony?

59. _____

60. Watching local high school basketball games (1)**has** (2)**have** become his favorite weekend activity.

60. _____

61. His baseball and his glove (1)**was** (2)**were** all Jamil was permitted to take to the game.

61. _____

62. Neither my friend nor I (1)**expects** (2)**expect** to go on the overnight trip.

62. _____

63. My coach and mentor (1)**is** (2)**are** Gwen Johnson.

63. _____

64. Cable television, along with VCRs and DVDs, (1)**has** (2)**have** drawn millions of viewers away from traditional network television.

64. _____

65. She is the only one of six candidates who (1)**refuses** (2)**refuse** to speak at the ceremony.

65. _____

66. Neither the systems analyst nor the accountants (1)**was** (2)**were** able to locate the problem in the computer program.

66. _____

29. SENTENCES AND GRAMMAR: Pronoun-Antecedent Agreement

(Study 127, Pronoun-Antecedent Agreement)

Write the number of the **correct** choice.

Example: One of the women fell from (1)**her** (2)**their** horse.   1

1. Agatha Christie is the kind of writer who loves to keep (1)**her** (2)**their** readers guessing until the last page.   1. _____

2. Many tourists traveling in the West enjoy stopping at roadside attractions because (1)**you** (2)**they** never know what to expect.   2. _____

3. When Lucia found that her young son had caught the measles, she became concerned that (1)**it** (2)**they** would leave marks on his face.   3. _____

4. He majored in mathematics because (1)**it** (2)**they** had always been of interest to him.   4. _____

5. Lucy edited the news because (1)**it was** (2)**they were** often full of inaccuracies.   5. _____

6. He assumed that all of his students had done (1)**his** (2)**their** best to complete the test.   6. _____

7. Both Ed and Luis decided to stretch (1)**his** (2)**their** legs when the bus reached Houston.   7. _____

8. Ironically, neither woman had considered how to make (1)**her** (2)**their** job easier.   8. _____

9. Each of the researchers presented (1)**a** (2)**their** theory about the age of the solar system.   9. _____

10. He buys his books at the campus bookstore because (1)**it has** (2)**they have** low prices.   10. _____

11. Electronics can be a rewarding field of study, because (1)**it** (2)**they** can lead to good jobs in a number of areas.   11. _____

12. Every member of the men's basketball team received (1)**his** (2)**their** individual trophy.   12. _____

13. All in the class voted to have (1)**its** (2)**their** term papers due a week earlier.   13. _____

14. I like swimming because it develops (1)**one's** (2)**your** muscles without straining the joints.   14. _____

15. Neither Aaron nor Marzell has declared (1)**his** (2)**their** major.   15. _____

16. Citizens who still do not recycle (1)**your** (2)**their** garbage need to read this news article.   16. _____

17. The Zoomation Company has just introduced (1)**its** (2)**their** new 300-gigabyte computer.   17. _____

18. Neither the guide nor the hikers seemed aware of (1)**her** (2)**their** danger on the trail.   18. _____

19. The faculty has already selected (1)**its** (2)**their** final candidates.   19. _____

20. Critics argue that (1)**those kind** (2)**those kinds** of movies may promote violent tendencies in children.   20. _____

21. One has to decide early in life what (1)**one wants** (2)**they want** out of life.   21. _____

22. Neither the coach nor the players underestimated (1)**her** (2)**their** opponents.   22. _____

23. The corporation insists that (1)**its** (2)**their** financial statements have been completely honest.   23. _____

24. Students should take accurate and complete notes so that (1)**they** (2)**you** will be prepared for the exam.   24. _____

25. Some people prefer trains to planes because trains bring (1)**you** (2)**them** closer to the scenery.   25. _____

26. In the next five years, owners of older vehicles polluting the environment can sell (1)**their** (2)**your** cars or trucks for scrap.

26. _____

27. If a stranger tried to talk to her, she would just look at (1)**him** (2)**them** and smile.

27. _____

28. Every one of the trees in the affected area had lost most of (1)**its** (2)**their** leaves.

28. _____

29. Some women can understand (1)**herself** (2)**themself** (3)**themselves** better through reading feminist literature.

29. _____

30. The medical committee was surprised to learn that (1)**its** (2)**their** preliminary findings had been published in the newspaper.

30. _____

31. The campus disciplinary board determined that (1)**its** (2)**their** process for reviewing student complaints was too cumbersome and slow.

31. _____

32. None of the boys should blame (1)**himself** (2)**themself** (3)**themselves** (4)**yourself** for misfortunes that cannot be prevented.

32. _____

33. Rita is a person who cannot control (1)**her** (2)**their** anger when under stress.

33. _____

34. Professor Brown is one of those teachers who really love (1)**his** (2)**their** profession.

34. _____

35. Everyone in the men's locker room grabbed (1)**his** (2)**their** clothes and ran when the cry of "Fire!" came from the hallway.

35. _____

36. Rita is the only one of the singers who writes (1)**her** (2)**their** own music.

36. _____

37. Each of the singers in the newly formed Irish band dreamed of earning (1)**her** (2)**their** first million dollars.

37. _____

38. As part of the Kim family's Vietnamese New Year celebration, each wrote *cau doi*. Memories of home and family are the subject of (1)**this kind of poem** (2)**these kind of poems**.

38. _____

39. During the Christmas season, many Latin American families serve (1)**its** (2)**their** favorite dish—tortillas spread with mashed avocado and roast chicken.

39. _____

40. If everyone in the Women's Club would contribute a small portion of (1)**her** (2)**their** January 1 paycheck, we should be able to purchase the microwave for the staff luncheon room.

40. _____

41. Each cat claimed (1)**its** (2)**their** specific area of the bedroom for long afternoon naps.

41. _____

42. Hearing-impaired people now have a telecommunication device to allow (1)**him** (2)**them** to make phone calls to a hearing person.

42. _____

43. When my professors complain that Americans don't support local school districts, I remind (1)**her** (2)**them** that most families view education as extremely important.

43. _____

44. Drivers of the new Mercolet sedan know that Mercolet has produced the most stylish car that (1)**its** (2)**their** engineers could design.

44. _____

45. If viewers are not happy with public television programming, (1)**you** (2)**they** should write letters to local television stations.

45. _____

46. Researchers have found that the type of relationship couples have can affect (1)**your** (2)**their** overall immune system.

46. _____

47. When climbing a mountain in autumn, amateurs had better take warm clothing in (1)**your** (2)**their** packs to guard against hypothermia.

47. _____

48. Unfortunately, Sid was one of those climbers who neglected to pack (1)**his** (2)**their** winter gear.

48. _____

49. A neighborhood organization of young people is meeting to determine how (1)**it** (2)**they** can help elderly neighbors in the community.

49. _____

50. Either the lead actor or the chorus members missed (1)**his** (2)**their** cue.

50. _____

30. SENTENCES AND GRAMMAR: Agreement Review

(Study 126–127, Agreement)

Write **C** if the sentence is **correct**.
Write **X** if it is **incorrect**.

Example: Nobody in the first two rows were singing.   _____X_____

1.   The deep blue of the waters seem to reflect the sky.   1. _____

2.   All of the fish swim upstream in spring.   2. _____

3.   All of the fish tastes good if you grill it properly.   3. _____

4.   The strength of these new space-age materials have been demonstrated many times.   4. _____

5.   All these experiences, along with the special love and care that my daughter needs, have taught me the value of caring.   5. _____

6.   Evan's pants are ripped beyond repair.   6. _____

7.   There's a northbound bus and a southbound bus that leave here every hour.   7. _____

8.   According to a recent survey, almost every American feels that their self-esteem is important.   8. _____

9.   The management now realizes that a bigger budget is needed; they plan to ask for federal assistance.   9. _____

10. When an older student senses that an institution understands nontraditional students, she generally works to her academic potential.   10. _____

11. I found that the thrill of attending college soon leaves when you have to visit the bursar's office.   11. _____

12. Everyone who read the letter stated that they were surprised by the contents.   12. _____

13. You should hire one of those experts who solves problems with computers.   13. _____

14. Two hundred miles was too much for a day trip.   14. _____

15. At school, there are constant noise and confusion at lunch.   15. _____

16. Cleveland or Cincinnati are planning to host the statewide contests.   16. _____

17. Bacon and eggs are no longer considered a healthy breakfast.   17. _____

18. Probably everybody in the computer center, except Colleen and Aaron, know how to run the scanner.   18. _____

19. Neither Chuck nor Arnold are as blessed with talent as Sylvester.   19. _____

20. *Powerpuff Girls* was described as "comic book stuff" by the newspaper's television critic.   20. _____

21. The researcher, as well as her assistants, are developing a study to compare the brain tissue of Alzheimer's disease sufferers and healthy subjects.   21. _____

22. Neither criticism nor frequent failures were enough to retard his progress.   22. _____

23. Where are the end of the recession and the revival of consumer confidence?   23. _____

24. Economics have been the most dismal science I've ever studied.   24. _____

25. Has either of your letters appeared in the newspaper?   25. _____

26. It were the general and the Secretary of State who finally convinced the President that an armed conflict might be inevitable.

26. _____

27. Neither Janet nor her parents seem interested in our offer to help.

27. _____

28. He is one of those employees who was always late for work on Monday mornings.

28. _____

29. She is the only one of the experts who solves problems with computers.

29. _____

30. The faculty are squabbling among themselves, disagreeing vehemently about Faculty Senate bylaws.

30. _____

31. Such was the hardships of the times that many were forced into begging or stealing to survive.

31. _____

32. The special scissors that was needed for the repair could not be found.

32. _____

33. Billiards were returning to popularity at the time.

33. _____

31. SENTENCES AND GRAMMAR: Effective Sentences

(Study 128, Creating Effective Sentences)

Choose the **most effective** way of expressing the given ideas. Write the letter of your choice (**A**, **B**, or **C**) in the blank.

Example: A. The floods came. They washed away the roadway. They also uprooted trees.

B. The floods came, and they washed away the roadway and uprooted trees.

C. The floods came, washing away the roadway and uprooting trees. ____C____

1. A. There was a company in Minneapolis. It shortened its work week from 40 hours to 36 hours. The company's output increased.

B. A company in Minneapolis shortened its work week from 40 hours to 36 hours, and this company found out the company's output increased.

C. When a Minneapolis company shortened its work week from 40 to 36 hours, its output increased. 1._____

2. A. Broadway has been revived by a new band of actors. These new actors are from Hollywood. They find it refreshing and challenging to perform before a live audience.

B. Broadway has been revived by a new breed of actors—Hollywood stars, who find it refreshing and challenging to perform before a live audience.

C. Broadway has been revived by this new breed of actors, which has seen actors coming from Hollywood; they have found it refreshing and challenging to perform before a live audience. 2._____

3. A. Recreational tree climbing has become popular. Ecologists hope that a code of tree-climbing ethics will be developed. Such a code may help to prevent damage to the delicate forest ecosystems.

B. Recreational tree climbing has become popular and ecologists hope that a code of tree-climbing ethics will be developed, and such a code may help to prevent damage to the delicate forest ecosystems.

C. Before recreational tree climbing becomes any more popular, ecologists hope that a code of tree-climbing ethics will be developed to prevent permanent damage to delicate forest ecosystems. 3._____

4. A. Harry Truman, who woke up the next morning to find himself elected President, had gone to bed early on election night.

   B. Harry Truman, who had gone to bed early on election night, woke up the next morning to find himself elected President.

   C. Harry Truman went to bed early on election night, and he woke up the next morning and found himself elected President.

   4. _____

5. A. The papers were marked "Top Secret." The term *Top Secret* indicates contents of extraordinary value.

   B. The papers were of extraordinary value, and therefore they were marked "Top Secret."

   C. The papers were marked "Top Secret," indicating their extraordinary value.

   5. _____

6. A. The university was noted for its outstanding faculty, its concern for minorities, and the quality of its graduates.

   B. The university was noted for its outstanding faculty, it showed concern for minorities, and how well its graduates did.

   C. The university was known for three things: it had an outstanding faculty, it showed concern for minorities, and the quality of its graduates.

   6. _____

7. A. The Broadway theater, which has survived many changes, is changing rapidly again, the change being that wealthy entertainment corporations, which include, for example, Disney's company, are taking over the big theaters as they bring in huge musicals that have vapid content, high prices, and draw audiences away from more challenging plays.

   B. The Broadway theater, having survived many changes, is again changing rapidly as wealthy entertainment corporations such as Disney's take over the big theaters with vapid, high-priced musicals, drawing audiences away from more challenging plays.

   C. The Broadway theater has survived many changes. Once again it is changing rapidly. Wealthy entertainment corporations are taking over the big theaters. One example is Disney. These corporations bring in huge musicals that prove to be vapid as well as high priced. The result is that they draw audiences away from more challenging plays.

   7. _____

8. A. Nick moves to Long Island and rents a house, and it is next to Gatsby's, but he does not know Gatsby. One night he sees a shadowy figure on the lawn, and he concludes that it must be Gatsby himself.

   B. Moving to Long Island, Nick rents a house next to Gatsby's. Though he does not know Gatsby, one night he concludes that the shadowy figure he sees on the lawn must be Gatsby himself.

   C. Nick, who moves to Long Island, rents a house which is next to Gatsby's, whom he does not know; one night he concludes that the shadowy figure that he sees on the lawn must be Gatsby himself.

8. _____

9. A. A fungus struck one plant and then another until it had killed nearly all of them, but one of them survived.

   B. A fungus that killed nearly all the plants spread from one to another, yet only one survived.

   C. A fungus spread among the plants, killing all but one.

9. _____

10. A. One family in a heatless building called the welfare office for money to buy an electric heater.

    B. One family lived in a building that had no heat, and so they called the welfare office to get money to buy an electric heater.

    C. One family, calling the welfare office for money to buy an electric heater, lived in a building that was heatless.

10. _____

32. SENTENCES AND GRAMMAR: Effective Sentences

(Study 128B–E, Use Coordination, Compounding, Subordination, Reduction)

Rewrite each of the following sets of sentences in the **most effective** way. Your result may contain one sentence or more. You may add, drop, or change words, but do not omit any information.

Example: The Lions had the ball on the Broncos' ten-yard line, and they attempted four passes, but they could not score, and so they lost the game.

Though the Lions had the ball on the Broncos' ten-yard line, they lost the game because they could not score in four pass attempts.

(Collaborative option: Students work in pairs or small groups to suggest different ways of rewriting.)

1. The Washington Monument was closed to the public. This happened in the spring and fall of 1998. The National Park Service had to repair the structure. That was the reason for the closing.

_____

_____

_____

_____

2. One airline charges an unrestricted fare of $1,734 from Boston to Reykjavik. Reykjavik is in Iceland. The same airline will fly you between the same cities for $298.

_____

_____

_____

_____

3. Many college students have a choice. This is what car-leasing companies report. These college students are the ones who do not have much in savings. One choice is that they can drive an old used car. The other is that they can lease a new car.

_____

_____

_____

_____

4. Computers have become less expensive. They have also become easier to use. And you can get free software. With this you can browse the Internet.

    _____

    _____

    _____

    _____

5. More bodies were pulled from the floodwaters in central Texas. This happened as storms continued their eastward march across the Southwest. The storms were torrential, and the march was deadly. One man was killed. This was because his home was swept away in the floods.

    _____

    _____

    _____

    _____

6. A new report has come out. It states that girls now outnumber boys in secondary schools. This is true in eighteen countries. Most of these countries are in Latin America.

    _____

    _____

    _____

    _____

7. But fifty-one countries still have serious gender gaps in education. In these countries there are 75 million fewer girls than boys in schools. This figure comes from a report by a population research group. The report was released on October 18.

    _____

    _____

    _____

    _____

8. The Surgeon General has announced new plans. The plans unveil the first national strategy for suicide prevention. The Surgeon General says that suicide is a serious public health problem, and it can no longer be ignored.

    _____

    _____

    _____

    _____

9. Gardeners are dealing with an increasingly serious pest. These gardeners are on both sides of the Rocky Mountains. The pest is hungry deer. Some gardeners are spraying odors. The deer do not like these odors. Other gardeners are covering their plants with plastic.

    _____

    _____

    _____

    _____

10. Kidnappings have reached record levels around the world. The global economic turmoil is likely to push the figure still higher. A leading institution states this.

    _____

    _____

    _____

    _____

33. SENTENCES AND GRAMMAR: Parallel Structure

(Study 128F, Use Parallel Structure)

Part 1

For each sentence: in the first three blanks, **identify** each of the boldfaced elements (use the abbreviations in parentheses):

gerund or gerund phrase (**ger**)	participle or participial phrase (**part**)
prepositional phrase (**prep**)	infinitive or infinitive phrase (**inf**)
clause (**cl**)	adjective (**adj**)
noun [with or without modifiers] (**noun**)	
verb [with or without modifiers or complements] (**verb**)	

Then, in the last blank, write **P** if the sentence contains **parallel structure**, or **NP** if it does **not**. (If the sentence is parallel, the first three blanks will all have the same answer.)

_____

Examples: Congress rushed **to pass the tax bill, the Medicare bill,
and to adjourn.**   _inf_   _noun_   _inf_   _NP_
Shakespeare was **a poet, a playwright, and an actor**.   _noun_   _noun_   _noun_   _P_

1. The job required some knowledge of **word processing, desktop
    publishing, and to write.**   1. _____ _____ _____ _____

2. Hector fought with **great skill, epic daring, and superb intelligence.** 2. _____ _____ _____ _____

3. The mosques of ancient Islamic Spain typically contained **ornate
    stone screens, long hallways, and the columns looked like spindles.** 3. _____ _____ _____ _____

4. The castle, **built on a hill, surrounded by farmland, and com-
    manding a magnificent view,** protected the peasants from invasions
    by hostile forces.   4. _____ _____ _____ _____

5. A newly discovered primate from the Amazon has **wide-set eyes, a
    broad nose, and the fur is striped like a zebra.**   5. _____ _____ _____ _____

6. By nightfall, we were **tired, hungry, and grumpy.**   6. _____ _____ _____ _____

7. The guerrillas **surrounded the village, set up their mortars, and
    the shelling began.**   7. _____ _____ _____ _____

8. Kiesha did not know **where she had come from, why she was
    there, or the time of her departure.**   8. _____ _____ _____ _____

9. Her favorite pastimes remain **designing clothes, cooking gourmet
    meals, and practicing the flute.**   9. _____ _____ _____ _____

10. Eliot's poetry is **witty, complex, and draws on his vast learning.** 10. _____ _____ _____ _____

Rewrite each sentence in parallel structure.

Example: The apartment could be rented by the week, the month, or you could pay on a yearly basis.
        The apartment could be rented by the week, month, or year.

(Collaborative option: Students work in pairs or small groups to explore possible different parallel options. Each student writes a different version—where possible—in the blanks.)

1. Before 8 a.m., my youngest son had made himself breakfast, a snow fort in the front yard, and tormented his brothers.

   _____

   _____

   _____

2. Our new wood-burning stove should keep us warm, save us money, and should afford us much pleasure.

   _____

   _____

   _____

3. Christopher Columbus has been remembered as an entrepreneur, an explorer, a sailor, and now perhaps for how he exploited native populations.

   _____

   _____

   _____

4. The chief ordered Agent 007 to break into the building, crack the safe, and to steal the plans.

   _____

   _____

   _____

5. A good batter knows how to hit to the opposite field and staring down the pitcher.

   _____

   _____

   _____

6. When kindergartners were asked how the U.S. President should behave, they said someone who was fair, who shares, and not a hitter.

_____

_____

_____

7. The scouts marched briskly off into the woods, trekked ten miles to Alder Lake, and tents were erected by them.

_____

_____

_____

8. Dean has three main strengths: his ability to listen, he likes people, and his interest in cultural awareness.

_____

_____

_____

9. Global warming may not only increase air and ocean temperatures but also the force of storms.

_____

_____

_____

10. Neither regulating prices nor wages will slow inflation enough.

_____

_____

_____

11. During its early years, Sears, Roebuck and Company sold not only clothes, furniture and hardware, but also customers could buy cars and houses.

_____

_____

_____

12. Charlene practiced shooting from the top of the key as well as how to dribble with either hand.

_____

_____

_____

13. The new ambassador impressed everyone with her wit, charm, her grace, and they liked her intelligence.

_____

_____

_____

14. The experimental group either consisted of white rats or gray ones.

_____

_____

_____

15. But in a larger sense we cannot dedicate this ground, we cannot consecrate it either, nor can it be hallowed by us.

_____

_____

_____

34. SENTENCES AND GRAMMAR: Fragments

(Study 129A, Fragments)

| Part 1 |

Write **S** after each item that is one or more **complete sentences.**
Write **F** after each item that contains a **fragment.**

Example: Luis was offered the job. Having presented the best credentials.   ____F____

1. When people enter a theater or house of worship. It is important for them to turn off their cell phones.   1. _____

2. Being coached in what is appropriate to do and say in a job interview, so as not to make a disastrous mistake.   2. _____

3. The manuscript having been returned, Johanna sat down to revise it.   3. _____

4. Harrison desperately wanted the part. Because he believed that this was the film that would make him a star.   4. _____

5. The old-fashioned clock stopped ticking. Renée had forgotten to wind it.   5. _____

6. He admitted to being a computer nerd. As a matter of fact, he was proud of his computing skills.   6. _____

7. More than 50 percent of Americans surveyed felt guilty about their child-care arrangements.   7. _____

8. I read all the articles. Then I wrote the first draft of my paper.   8. _____

9. Many Americans prefer indirect business levies rather than direct taxation. Where do you stand on this issue?   9. _____

10. Maurice kept nodding his head as the coach explained the play. Thinking all the time that it would never work.   10. _____

11. Because she was interested in rocks, she majored in geology.   11. _____

12. I argued with two of my classmates. First with Edward and then with Harry.   12. _____

13. There are many humorous research projects. Such as developing an artificial dog to breed fleas for allergy studies.   13. _____

14. Taylor was absolutely positive he would pass. Regardless of having received failing grades on both his essay and the midterm.   14. _____

15. Colleen stepped up to the free-throw line; then she made two points to win the game.   15. _____

16. Professor Fustie was known for his forgetfulness. For example, leaving his grade book in the men's room.   16. _____

17. Because the army could not indefinitely maintain such a long supply line.   17. _____

18. She went to the supermarket. After she had made a list of groceries that she needed.   18. _____

19. I telephoned Dr. Gross. The man who had been our family physician for many years.   19. _____

20. We suspect Harry of the theft. Because he had access to the funds and he has been living far beyond his means.   20. _____

Rewrite each item in one or more sentences, eliminating any **fragment(s)**. You may add information, but do not omit any.

Examples: Chief Joseph led his Native Americans on a desperate flight to freedom. A flight doomed to failure.
Chief Joseph led his Native Americans on a desperate flight to freedom, a flight doomed to failure.

Because the patient was near death.
Because the patient was near death, the doctors operated immediately.

(Collaborative option: Students work in pairs or small groups to suggest different ways of rewriting.)

1. Two days before the competition, he felt nervous. However, much more at ease just before the contest.

_____

_____

_____

2. She was a star athlete. A brilliant student besides.

_____

_____

_____

3. If there is no change in the patient's condition within the next twenty-four hours.

_____

_____

_____

4. The Scottish and Irish farmers forced from their land so it could be turned into sheep pastures. More profitable for the landowners.

_____

_____

_____

5. When it becomes too hot to work in the fields. The workers taking a welcomed rest.

_____

_____

_____

35. SENTENCES AND GRAMMAR: Comma Splices and Fused Sentences

(Study 129B, Comma Splices and Fused Sentences)

Part 1

Write **S** after any item that is a **complete sentence**.
Write **Spl** after any item that is a **comma splice**.
Write **FS** after any item that is a **fused sentence**.

Example: The mission was a success, everyone was pleased.   _____Spl_____

1. The apartment was up two rickety flights of stairs it was the best they could afford.   1._____

2. The party broke up at one in the morning, Jack lingered for a few final words with Kathy.   2._____

3. Battered by insider-trading scandals, the stock market plunged to its yearly low.   3._____

4. The moon enters the earth's shadow, a lunar eclipse occurs, causing the moon to turn a deep red.   4._____

5. The ticket agent had sold eighty-one tickets to boarding passengers there were only eleven
   empty seats on the train.   5._____

6. Since she was in the mood for a romantic comedy, she hired a babysitter and went to see the
   film *Last Holiday.*   6._____

7. Sheer exhaustion having caught up with me, I had no trouble falling asleep.   7._____

8. The restaurant check almost made me faint, because I had left my wallet home, I couldn't pay
   for the meal.   8._____

9. Those of us who lived in off-campus housing ignored the rule, since we were seniors, we never
   worried about campus regulations.   9._____

10. It was a cloudy, sultry afternoon when we sighted our first school of whales, and the cry of
    "Lower the boats!" rang throughout the ship.   10._____

11. The war was finally over; however, little could be done to ease the refugees' sense of loss.   11._____

12. The author described fifty ways to recycle fruitcakes; my favorite is to use slices of fruitcake as
    drink coasters.   12._____

13. The three major television networks face stiff competition for ratings, because of cable networks,
    viewers can decide from among four hundred programs.   13._____

14. In the film a lawyer reopens an investigation on behalf of a woman imprisoned for murder she
    convincingly claims that she is innocent.   14._____

15. Though the teacher believed that it was important for her students to write every day, she did
    not enjoy grading so many papers.   15._____

Rewrite each item in one or more **correct sentences,** eliminating any **comma splices** or **fused sentences.** Add or change words as needed. Do not omit any information.

Example: The software game was full of violent scenes, thus it was banned from the school's computer center.
The software game was banned from the school's computer center because it was full of violent scenes.

(Collaborative option: Students work in pairs or small groups to suggest different ways of rewriting.)

1. Some Americans are still buying sport-utility vehicles, however, they are finding the insurance premiums unexpectedly high.

   _____

   _____

   _____

2. Crime is still a major concern for many Americans so many teenagers are arrested for violent crimes.

   _____

   _____

   _____

3. I waited in line for my turn at the automatic teller machine, I balanced my checkbook.

   _____

   _____

   _____

4. Over 30 percent of children from rural America live in mobile homes, therefore, Congress has established a commission to study mobile home safety and construction standards.

   _____

   _____

   _____

5. A shortage of licensed contractors often exists in the areas hit by natural disasters homeowners quickly learn to wait for a work crew with the proper credentials.

   _____

   _____

   _____

6. The largest Native American reservation is the Navajo it is located mostly in Arizona and covers 16 million acres.

_____

_____

_____

7. According to some researchers, little boys may have different educational experiences from little girls, in other words, even though it may be unintentional, teachers often have subtly different expectations based on the gender of their students.

_____

_____

_____

_____

8. Tarantulas are large spiders with powerful fangs and a mean bite, they live not only in the tropics but also in the United States.

_____

_____

_____

9. Jogging can reduce fatal heart attacks because it is an aerobic activity, it keeps the arteries from clogging.

_____

_____

_____

10. The software game was full of violent scenes, therefore, it was banned from the school's computer center. [Correct this in a different way from that shown in the example.]

_____

_____

_____

36. SENTENCES AND GRAMMAR: Fragments, Comma Splices, and Fused Sentences

(Study 129, Conquering the "Big Three" Sentence Errors)

Rewrite any item that contains a **fragment**, **comma splice**, or **fused sentence**, so that it contains none of these. You may add words or information as needed, but do not omit any information. If an item is already correct, leave the blank empty.

Examples: When she saw the full moon rising over the hill.
     When she saw the full moon rising over the hill, she thought of the night they had met.
     When Peary and Henson reached the Pole, they rejoiced.

(Collaborative option: Students work in pairs or small groups to suggest different ways of rewriting.)

1. Because pie, ice cream, and candy bars have practically no nutritional value.

_____

_____

_____

2. When the bindings release, the ski comes off.

_____

_____

_____

3. Which promotes tooth decay when not used properly.

_____

_____

_____

4. Lady Bird Johnson and Barbara Bush, first ladies greatly admired.

_____

_____

_____

5. Whereas older cars run on leaded gas and lack complex pollution controls.

_____

_____

_____

6. Because she was not prepared for the interviewer's questions and felt she would never get the job.

_____

_____

_____

7. By installing smoke detectors, families may someday save family members from perishing in a fire.

_____

_____

_____

8. Watching from the seventh floor during the parade.

_____

_____

_____

9. Which could strengthen your immune system.

_____

_____

_____

10. Stay.

_____

_____

_____

11. We planned the trip carefully, yet we still had a series of disasters.

_____

_____

_____

12. The quarterback signed the largest professional football contract to date, he will earn $120 million over a six-year period.

_____

_____

_____

13. Native Americans dances and music for every tribal ceremony and social occasion celebrated.

_____

_____

_____

14. Scientists are currently interested in studying polar bears. Because the bears' body chemistry may reveal how pollution has affected the Arctic.

_____

_____

_____

15. Americans, for the moment, may be less concerned about taxes. Polls indicate that Americans would rather balance the federal budget than lower taxes.

_____

_____

_____

16. Until all the workers were able to present their points of view.

_____

_____

_____

17. The community was unaware of the city's plan to tear down a playground, therefore, few citizens attended the city council meetings.

_____

_____

_____

18. Since 1975, over 1.5 million Vietnamese have left their homeland in search of a peaceful life, many have settled in Australia, Canada, Europe, and the United States.

_____

_____

_____

19. Because the founder of a popular fast-food restaurant chain has encouraged corporations to provide financial support for employees adopting children.

———————————————————————————————

———————————————————————————————

———————————————————————————————

20. All my coworkers on diets and won't eat any cookies or cake.

———————————————————————————————

———————————————————————————————

———————————————————————————————

21. What happened to Clyde, Roberta, and Sondra is told in the novel *An American Tragedy* it was written by Theodore Dreiser.

———————————————————————————————

———————————————————————————————

———————————————————————————————

22. He wore a pair of mud-encrusted, flap-soled boots they looked older than he did.

———————————————————————————————

———————————————————————————————

———————————————————————————————

23. For the agency wanted to know how its money was spent.

———————————————————————————————

———————————————————————————————

———————————————————————————————

24. Enrique reread his assignment a dozen times before handing it in. To be absolutely sure his ideas were clear.

———————————————————————————————

———————————————————————————————

———————————————————————————————

25. The executive waited, however, until every worker at the meeting presented a point of view.

———————————————————————————————

———————————————————————————————

———————————————————————————————

26. That she is dead is beyond dispute.

_____

_____

_____

27. "I believe," declared the headmaster. "That you deserve expulsion."

_____

_____

_____

28. The scouts hiked two miles until they reached the falls then they had lunch.

_____

_____

_____

29. The police having been warned to expect trouble, every available officer lined the avenue of the march.

_____

_____

_____

30. In the 1800s, Ireland's vital crop was wiped out by the potato blight, Irish people who owned ten acres of land were disqualified from poor relief.

_____

_____

_____

31. The Irish immigrants did not settle on farms for fear that the potato blight would strike again, but the German immigrants did go into farming they had no fear of this blight.

_____

_____

_____

32. In the first George Bush's administration the Gulf War, and in George W. Bush's the war against terrorism.

_____

_____

_____

33. A victory that is unmatched in the history of amateur sports.

_____

_____

_____

37. SENTENCES AND GRAMMAR: Placement of Sentence Parts

(Study 130A, Needless Separation of Related Sentence Parts)

If the boldfaced words are **in the wrong place**, draw an arrow from these words to the place in the sentence where they should be.

If the boldfaced words are **in the right place**, do nothing.

Examples: Never give a toy to a child **that can be swallowed**.

People who buy cigars **made in Cuba** violate U.S. laws.

1. He ordered a pizza for his friends **covered with pepperoni.**

2. She **only** had enough money to buy two of the three books that she needed.

3. The parents of college students **who have earned scholarships** are indeed fortunate.

4. After asking a few questions, we decided **quickly** to end the conference call because we

   weren't interested in what the company had to offer.

5. We saw the plane taxi onto the field **that would soon be leaving for Chicago.**

6. Some Americans are spending **almost** a third of their income on rent.

7. The President attempted to prevent the outbreak of war **in the Oval Office.**

8. Unfortunately, the resale shop was full of **wrinkled** little girls' dresses.

9. We hurriedly bought a picnic table from a clerk **with collapsible legs.**

10. We learned that no one could discard anything at the municipal dump **except people living**

    in the community.

11. The only baseball jacket left was a **green and white** child's starter jacket.

12. The race car driver planned **after the Grand Prix race** to retire before she received another injury.

13. The bride walked down the aisle with her father **wearing her mother's wedding gown.**

14. Despite her sincerity and honesty, the candidate failed to **carefully, completely, and with candor** explain why she dropped out of the campaign.

15. The two scientists, **working independently,** achieved the same results.

16. Send, **after you have received all the donations,** the total amount to the organization's headquarters.

17. **Only** one teacher seems able to convince Raymond that he should study.

18. Only a few Olympic athletes can expect lucrative endorsement contracts **with gold medals**.

19. We watched the *Queen Elizabeth II* as she slowly sailed out to sea **from our hotel window**.

20. Indicate **on the enclosed sheet** whether you are going to the class picnic.

21. A **battered** man's hat was hanging on a branch of the tree.

22. Sam, **running out in his robe and slippers to get the morning newspaper on a cold January morning,** slammed the front door shut and then realized that he was locked out.

23. Croaker College, which had **almost** lost all of its football games last year, fired its coach.

24. Albino Ruales realized **when he heard that his grandmother was moving in with his family** that many households are now multigenerational.

25. He replied that they went to Paris **usually** in the spring.

38. SENTENCES AND GRAMMAR: Dangling and Misplaced Modifiers

(Study 130A, Needless Separation of Related Sentence Parts, and 130B, Dangling Modifiers)

| Part 1 |

If the boldfaced words are a dangling or misplaced modifier, **rewrite** the sentence correctly in the blanks below it. If the sentence is correct, do nothing.

Examples: **Returning the corrected essays**, most students were disappointed by their marks.
     When the instructor returned their corrected essays, most students were disappointed by their marks.

     Roosevelt and Churchill, **meeting at sea**, drafted the Four Freedoms.
     _____
     _____

(Collaborative option: Students work in pairs to suggest different ways of rewriting.)

1. **Announcing his first baseball game in 1939,** the late Red Barber began a broadcasting career that would last over fifty years.

   _____

   _____

   _____

2. **Rowing across the lake,** the moon often disappeared behind the clouds.

   _____

   _____

3. **Having worked on my paper for three hours,** the network went down and my paper was lost in cyberspace.

   _____

   _____

4. **While on vacation,** the idea for a new play came to him.

   _____

   _____

5. **Worried about what books their children are borrowing from libraries,** the library finally agreed to develop an on-line rating system for families.

   _____

   _____

   _____

6. **Upon entering college,** he applied for part-time employment in the library.

_____

_____

7. **Practicing every day for five hours,** Dani's expensive music lessons really paid off.

_____

_____

8. **Sleeping in late,** the house seemed incredibly quiet with the boys still in bed.

_____

_____

9. **After sleeping in until noon,** the day seemed to go by too quickly.

_____

_____

10. **When nine years old,** my father took my sister and me on our first camping trip.

_____

_____

11. **At the age of ten,** I was permitted to go, for the first time, to a summer camp.

_____

_____

12. **After putting away my fishing equipment,** the surface of the lake became choppy.

_____

_____

13. **Racing toward the primate section of the zoo,** the chimpanzees' playful laughter drew the children to their cage.

_____

_____

14. **To achieve a goal,** a person must expect to work and to make sacrifices.

_____

_____

15. **Suggesting that the American standard of living has declined,** some American economists predict a gloomy financial status for the next generation.

   _____

   _____

16. **After hearing of Tom's need for financial aid,** a hundred dollars was put at his disposal.

   _____

   _____

17. **Pickled in spiced vinegar,** the host thought the peaches would go with the meat.

   _____

   _____

18. **While running in a local marathon,** the weather was quite uncooperative.

   _____

   _____

19. **Relieved by her high grade on the first paper,** her next paper seemed less difficult.

   _____

   _____

20. **To be a happy puppy,** you need to exercise your pet regularly.

   _____

   _____

21. **As a teenager,** Darlene worked two jobs to help her family financially.

   _____

   _____

22. **After eating too much chocolate,** my scale revealed that I had gained ten pounds.

   _____

   _____

23. Finally, **after working for days,** the garden was free of weeds.

   _____

   _____

24. **To proofread my paper,** I reread it several times and used the grammar- and spell-checking functions of my word-processing software.

_____

_____

25. **After finishing my assignment,** the dog ate it.

_____

_____

26. **To get ready for summer vacation,** camp registrations had to be completed this week.

_____

_____

27. **Realizing that the unemployment rate was still over 10 percent,** most workers were not changing jobs.

_____

_____

28. **To get a passing grade in this course,** the professor's little quirks must be considered.

_____

_____

Part 2

In the first set of blanks, write a sentence of your own containing a humorous dangling or misplaced modifier. In the second set of blanks, **rewrite** the sentence correctly.

Example: _Hanging stiffly from the clothesline, Mother saw that the wash had frozen overnight._
Mother saw that the wash, hanging stiffly from the clothesline, had frozen overnight.

(Collaborative option: Students work in pairs or small groups to invent and correct sentences.)

1. _____

_____

_____

_____

_____

_____

2.

3.

4.

5.

39. SENTENCES AND GRAMMAR: Effective Sentences Review

(Study 128–130, Effective Sentences)

If an item is **incorrect** or **ineffective** in any of the ways you learned in sections 128–130, **rewrite** it correctly or more effectively in the blanks below it.

If an item is **correct** and **effective** as is, do nothing.

_____

Examples: The lakes were empty of fish. Acid rain had caused this.
        <u>Acid rain had left the lakes empty of fish.</u>
    Working in pairs, the students edited each other's writing.

_____

(Collaborative option: Students work in pairs to suggest ways of rewriting incorrect or ineffective sentences.)

1. If one drives a car without thinking, you are more than likely to have an accident.

   _____

   _____

2. The entire class was so pleased at learning that Dr. Turner has rescheduled the quiz.

   _____

   _____

3. The author decided to forthrightly, absolutely, unequivocally, and immediately deny the allegations of plagiarism.

   _____

   _____

4. A study revealed that vigorous exercise may add only one or two years to a person's life. This study used Harvard graduates.

   _____

   _____

   _____

5. The film director, thinking only about how he could get the shot of the erupting volcano, endangered everyone.

   _____

   _____

6. With her new auditory implant, Audrey heard so much better.

_____

_____

7. Watching the star hitter blast a home run over the fence, the ball smashed a windshield of an expensive sports car.

_____

_____

8. The owner of the team seems to insult her players and fans and mismanaging the finances.

_____

_____

9. The witness walked into the courtroom, and then she wishes she could avoid testifying.

_____

_____

10. An increase in energy taxes causes most people to consider carpooling and improving energy-conservation practices in their homes.

_____

_____

_____

11. According to historians, settlers traveling westward used prairie schooners, not Conestoga wagons, and they used oxen and mules instead of horses to pull the wagons, and they did not pull their wagons into a circle when under an attack.

_____

_____

_____

_____

12. He told me that he was going to write a letter and not to disturb him.

_____

_____

13. Ajay Smith is a senior, and he just won national recognition for his poetry.

_____

_____

14. In the 1400s many English villages held football competitions, an inflated animal bladder was kicked or shoved

between two distant points by opposing teams.

_____

_____

_____

15. If a student knows how to study, you should achieve success.

_____

_____

16. He went to his office. He sat down. He opened his briefcase. He read some papers.

_____

_____

17. Summer is a time for parties, friendships, for sports, and in which we can relax.

_____

_____

18. I met the new dorm counselor in my oldest pajamas.

_____

_____

19. Being a ski jumper requires nerves of steel, you have to concentrate to the utmost, and being perfectly coordinated.

_____

_____

_____

20. The plane neither had enough fuel nor proper radar equipment.

_____

_____

21. The instructor wondered when did the students begin sneaking out of class.

_____

_____

22. Because they would not worship the Roman gods meant that Christians might be thrown to the lions.

_____

_____

23. In baseball, a sacrifice is when the batter allows himself to be put out in order to advance a base runner.

_____

_____

24. Saddened by the collapse of his marriage, Fassbinder's mansion now seemed an ugly, echoing cavern.

_____

_____

25. By the coach putting Robinson at quarterback would have given the team a chance at the title.

_____

_____

40. SENTENCES AND GRAMMAR: Review

(Study 101–130, Sentences and Grammar)

Part 1

Write **T** for each statement that is **true**.
Write **F** for each statement that is **false**.

Example: A **present participle** ends in -*ing* and is used as an adjective. _____T_____

1. Both a **gerund** and a **present participle** end in -*ing*. 1._____
2. The greatest number of words ever used in a **verb** is four. 2._____
3. **Parallel structure** is used to designate ideas that are unequal in importance. 3._____
4. A **dangling participle** may be corrected by being changed into a dependent clause. 4._____
5. *It's* is a contraction of *it is; its* is the **possessive** form of the pronoun *it*. 5._____
6. The **verb precedes the subject** in a sentence beginning with the expletive *there*. 6._____
7. A **preposition** may contain two or more words; *because of* is an example. 7._____
8. The **principal parts of a verb** are the *present tense*, the *future tense*, and the *past participle*. 8._____
9. A **collective noun** may be followed by either a singular or plural verb. 9._____
10. A **prepositional phrase** may be used only as an adjective modifier. 10._____
11. A **compound sentence** is one that contains two or more independent clauses. 11._____
12. Not all **adverbs** end in -*ly*. 12._____
13. The verb **be** is like an equal sign in mathematics. 13._____
14. A **noun clause** may be introduced by the subordinating conjunction *although*. 14._____
15. An **adjective clause** may begin with *when* or *where*. 15._____
16. Both **verbals** and **verbs** may have modifiers and complements. 16._____
17. The terminal punctuation of a declarative sentence is the **exclamation point.** 17._____
18. *Without* is a **subordinating conjunction**. 18._____
19. A sentence may begin with the word *because*. 19._____
20. The **verb** of a sentence can consist of a past participle alone. 20._____
21. A **subjective complement** may be a noun, a pronoun, or an adverb. 21._____
22. A **direct object** may be a noun or a pronoun. 22._____
23. When there is an **indirect object**, it must precede the direct object. 23._____
24. When there is an **objective complement**, it must precede the direct object. 24._____
25. Pronouns used as appositives are called **intensive pronouns.** 25._____
26. The word *scissors* takes a **singular verb**. 26._____
27. An **antecedent** is the noun for which a pronoun stands. 27._____

28. A **simple sentence** contains two or more independent clauses. 28. _____

29. A pronoun following the verb *be* needs the **objective case**. 29. _____

30. A **complex sentence** contains at least one independent clause and one dependent clause. 30. _____

31. A **sentence fragment** is not considered a legitimate unit of expression; a **nonsentence** is. 31. _____

32. **Adjectives** never stand next to the words they modify. 32. _____

33. Not all words ending in *-ly* are **adverbs**. 33. _____

34. An **indefinite pronoun** designates no particular person. 34. _____

35. The words *have* and *has* identify the **present perfect tense** of a verb. 35. _____

36. A statement with a subject and a verb can be a fragment if it follows a **subordinating conjunction**. 36. _____

37. An **adverb** may modify a noun, an adjective, or another adverb. 37. _____

38. **Verbs** are words that assert an action or a state of being. 38. _____

39. The **indicative mood** of a verb is used to express a command or a request. 39. _____

40. The function of a **subordinating conjunction** is to join a dependent clause to a main clause. 40. _____

41. The **subjunctive mood** expresses doubt, uncertainty, a wish, or a supposition. 41. _____

42. An **adjective** may modify a noun, a pronoun, or an adverb. 42. _____

43. A **gerund** is a verb form ending in *-ing* and used as a noun. 43. _____

44. A **clause** differs from a **phrase** in that a clause always has a subject and a predicate. 44. _____

45. **Adjectives** tell *what kind, how many,* or *which one;* **adverbs** tell *when, where, how,* and *to what degree.* 45. _____

46. A **comma splice** is a grammatical error caused by joining two independent clauses with a comma. 46. _____

47. **Coordinating conjunctions** *(and, but, or, nor, for, yet, so)* join words, phrases, and clauses of equal importance. 47. _____

48. **Pronouns in the objective case** *(him, me, . . .)* should be used as direct objects of verbs and verbals. 48. _____

49. **Mixed construction** occurs when two sections of a sentence that should be grammatically compatible are not. 49. _____

50. A **simple short sentence** can be a forceful expression in a passage. 50. _____

Part 2

Write **C** if the item is **correct**.
Write **X** if it is **incorrect**.

Example: Was that letter sent to Paul or **I**? _____X_____

1. **Having been notified to come at once,** there was no opportunity to call you. 1. _____

2. I suspected that his remarks were directed to Larry and **me**. 2. _____

3. He, **thinking that he might find his friends on the second floor of the library,** hurried. 3. _____

4. If a student attends the review session, **they** will do well on the first exam. 4. _____

5. In the cabin of the boat **was** a radio, a set of flares, and a map of the area. 5. _____

6. The Queen, standing beside her husband, children, and grandchildren, **were** waving regally at the crowd.

6. _____

7. She is a person **who** I think is certain to succeed as a social worker.

7. _____

8. **Is** there any other questions you wish to ask regarding the assignment?

8. _____

9. The driver had neglected to fasten his seat belt, **an omission that cost him a month in the hospital.**

9. _____

10. He particularly enjoys **playing softball** and **to run** a mile every morning.

10. _____

11. Forward the complaint to **whoever** you think is in charge.

11. _____

12. Every girl and boy **was** to have an opportunity to try out for the soccer team.

12. _____

13. Neither the bus driver nor the passengers **were** aware of their danger.

13. _____

14. Within the next five years, personal computers will be **not only** smaller **but also** more affordable.

14. _____

15. Not everyone feels that **their** life is better since the 1960s civil rights movement.

15. _____

16. Homemade bread tastes **differently** from bakery bread.

16. _____

17. Not **having had** the chance to consult his lawyer, Larry refused to answer the officer's questions.

17. _____

18. **Is** either of your friends interested in going to Florida over spring break?

18. _____

19. He enrolled in economics because **it** had always been of interest to him.

19. _____

20. The snow fell **steady** for two days.

20. _____

21. Burt paced nervously up and down the corridor. **Because he was concerned about the weather.**

21. _____

22. **A heavy rain began without warning,** the crew struggled with the tarpaulin.

22. _____

23. **To have better control over spending,** the checkbook is balanced each week.

23. _____

24. Casey **asked for time, stepped out of the batter's box, and his finger was pointed** toward the bleachers.

24. _____

25. **By investing in real estate at this time** can earn you a substantial profit in several years.

25. _____

41. SENTENCES AND GRAMMAR: Review

(Study 101–130, Sentences and Grammar)

On your own paper, **rewrite** each of the following paragraphs so that it is **free of errors** and more **effective**. You may change or reduce wording, combine sentences, and make any other necessary changes, but do not omit any information.

(Collaborative option: Students work in pairs or small groups to suggest ways of improving the paragraphs. They evaluate or edit each other's work.)

1. Neither the strength nor the wisdom of Clyde Griffiths' parents were sufficient to bring up their family properly. He grew ashamed of his parents, his clothes, and he had to live in ugly surroundings. Clyde grew older, he dreamed of a life of wealth and elegance. Spending most of his money on clothes and luxuries for himself, his parents were neglected by him. One night when Clyde's uncle invited him to dinner. He met beautiful, wealthy Sondra Finchley. Determined to have her, she was too far above his social position. So Clyde starts going with a factory worker, her name was Roberta, and she became pregnant by him, but it was decided by Clyde that just because of Roberta was no reason he had to give up his pursuit of Sondra.

2. The novel *Slaughterhouse-Five* tells of a man named Billy Pilgrim, who is a prisoner in World War II and later traveled to the planet Tralfamadore. In one particularly amusing episode, the Tralfamadoreans throw Billy into a cage in one of their zoos, along with a sexy Earthling actress named Montana Wildhack. The Tralfamadoreans crowd around the cage to watch the lovemaking between he and her. The less interesting sections of the novel depict the middle-class civilian life of Billy. Who grows wealthy despite having little awareness of what is going on. Billy acquires his wealth by becoming an optometrist, he marries his employer's daughter, and giving lectures on his space travels. I like most of the book because its the most unique novel I have ever read and because it makes you realize the horrors of war and the hollowness of much of American life. However, after reading the entire book, Kurt Vonnegut, Jr., the author, disappointed me because I, enjoying science fiction, wish they had put more about space travel into it.

3. In reading, critical comprehension differs from interpretive comprehension. Critical comprehension adds a new element. That element was judgment. On the interpretive level a student may understand that the author of a poem intends a flower to represent youth, on the critical level they evaluate the author's use of this symbol. The student evaluate the quality of the poem too. For example. On the interpretive level a student would perceive that the theme of a story is "If at first you don't succeed, try, try again"; on the critical level the student judges whether the saying is valid. Critical comprehension includes not only forming opinions about characters in stories but also judgments about them. By learning to comprehend critically, the student's overall reading ability will increase markedly.

4. Studying the woodland ground with my magnifying glass, I grew astonished. First I saw a column of tiny leaves marching along a two-inch-wide road. Peering through the glass, each leaf was being carried like an umbrella in the jaws of an ant far more smaller than the leaf itself. I began to notice other ant trails, all leading to tiny mounds of earth, they looked like miniature volcanoes. Up the mounds and into the craters trod endless parades of ants, each holding aloft its own parasol, which made my spine tingle with excitement. When I heard a faint buzzing made me look around. Above the ant-roads swarmed squadrons of tiny flies. As if on signal they dived straight down to attack the ants. If a person saw this, they would not have believed it. The ants, their jaws clamped upon the giant leaves, had no means of defense. Yet, as if answering air-raid sirens, you could see an army of smaller ants racing toward the leaf-carriers, who they strove to protect.

5. Because the leaf-carrying ants now had some protection did not mean that the attack was over by the flies. As the first attacking fly dived upon a leaf-carrier, the tiny protector ants reached and snapped at the aerial raider with their formidable jaws and they drove it away, but then all along the leaf-carrying column other flies joined the attack. Now I could see that atop each moving leaf a tiny protector ant was "riding shotgun" through my magnifying glass. Whenever a fly dive-bombed a leaf-carrier was when the shotgun ant on the leaf reached out and bit the fly. One shotgun ant grasped a fly's leg in its jaws and sends the winged enemy spinning to the ground. The ant's comrades swarmed all over the helpless fly, and it was soon reduced to a lifeless shell by them. Similar scenes were taken place all over the miniature battlefield. Finally the squadrons of flies, unable to penetrate the ants' defenses, rised, seemingly in formation, and droned back to their base. Would they mourn their casualties, I wondered. Will their leader have to report the failed attack to an angry insect general?

42. SENTENCES AND GRAMMAR: Review for Non-Native English Speakers

**(Study 107, Words that Connect; 115, Principal Parts of Verbs; and
120, Using Articles and Determiners Correctly)**

Part 1

In each ⎡box⎤ , write the **correct** preposition: **at**, **in**, or **on**.

On each blank line, write the **correct** verb ending: **ed** (or **d**), **s** (or **es**), or **ing**. If no ending is needed, leave
the line empty.

In each set of brackets [   ], write the correct **article**: **a**, **an**, or **the**. If no article is needed, leave the
brackets empty.

Example: [The] newest building ⎡ in ⎤ our city is [an] apartment house. It was constructed for senior citizens.

1. Living ⎡   ⎤ [   ] large city requires strong nerves and [   ] outstanding sense of humor. This is especially

   true ⎡   ⎤ Mondays. When I wait ⎡   ⎤ my corner for [   ] bus that take____ me to work, I hear [   ]

   screams of ambulances and fire engine____ as they speed by. When I am finally ⎡   ⎤ my office building, I am

   push____ into [   ] elevator by [   ] crowd. I manage to get off ⎡   ⎤ [   ] twelfth floor. But when I

   give [   ] cheery "Good morning!" to [   ] first coworker I meet, I am often answer____ with [   ]

   grouchy remark. The people at my former job, ⎡   ⎤ 1999, treat____ me much better. I stay____ there only a

   year, but it was [   ] best job I have had since be____ [   ] America.

2. In [   ] depth of winter ⎡   ⎤ 1925, ⎡   ⎤ [   ] small Alaskan town called Nome, [   ] epidemic of

   [   ] deadly disease diphtheria start____. The people were shock____ to hear that there was no medicine avail-

   able to stop [   ] disease from spread____. The ice-locked town was completely block____ off from the outside

   world: no boat or plane could reach____ it, and no roads or rail lines had yet been construct____ there. Only [   ]

   dogsleds might possibly rush____ the medicine to Nome in time. But [   ] nearest supply of medicine was

   ⎡   ⎤ the city of Anchorage, a thousand miles away. ⎡   ⎤ Nome's tiny telegraph office, the town's doctor trans-

   mitt____ [   ] desperate message: "Nome need____ diphtheria medicine at once!"

3. Officials in Anchorage round____ up all the available medicine and had it shipped ☐ [   ] train to the end

of the line ☐ Nenana, still 674 miles from Nome. From there relays of dogsled teams took over. The first

team's drivers trudge____ through the white wilderness to [   ] tiny hamlets of Tolovana and Bluff. ☐

Bluff, Gunnar Kaasen's team, headed by the dog Balto, began [   ] next leg of [   ] journey. Through raging

blizzards, thirty-below-zero cold, and missed relay stations, [   ] Balto led Kaasen's team all the way to Nome.

☐ just 5½ days the dog teams had cover____ what was normally [   ] month's journey. Nome had been

save____.

Part 2

In each blank, write any correct determiner (limiting adjective) from the list. Try not to use any word on the list more than once.

every	many	other	more	some	several
each	most	such	(a) little	another	all
(n) either	(a) few	both	much	enough	any

Example: They needed _another_ person to help lift the car.

_____ day last week there were _____ alarming stories in the newspapers.

_____ of them made _____ sense. One story said that soon there would not be

_____ fish left in the oceans or lakes. _____ story warned that global warming would

soon drown or boil us all. _____ of these stories gave me nightmares.

43. PUNCTUATION: The Comma

(Study 201–203, The Comma)

Part 1

If **no comma** is needed in the bracketed space(s), leave the blank empty. If **one or more commas** are needed, write in the **reason** from the list below (only one reason per blank; use the abbreviations in parentheses).

independent clauses joined by
   conjunction (**ind**)
introductory adverb clause (**intro**)
series (**ser**)
parenthetical expression (**par**)
nonrestrictive clause (**nr**)

appositive (**app**)
absolute phrase (**abs**)
direct address (**add**)
mild interjection (**inter**)
direct quotation (**quot**)

Examples: The New England states include Vermont[   ] Maine[   ] and New Hampshire.   _____ser_____
         The Secretary of State[   ] held a press conference.   _____

1. *The Gardens of Kyoto*[ ] a novel by Kate Walbert[ ] recounts a woman's coming of age in America, Paris, and Japan during the 1950s.   1. _____

2. Professors[   ] who assign too many long papers[   ] may have small classes.   2. _____

3. Well[ ] it looks as if I'll have to go to plan B.   3. _____

4. If the new security system fails to work[ ] we could be in deep trouble.   4. _____

5. In truth[ ] Dr. Faust[ ] your future does not look good.   5. _____

6. Phillip's father[   ] who is a religious man[   ] disapproves of many teenage antics.   6. _____

7. Dan and Marilyn[   ] however[   ] are hopeful for a 2008 victory.   7. _____

8. John Fitzgerald Kennedy[   ] the thirty-fifth President of the United States[   ] was assassinated on November 22, 1963.   8. _____

9. The Chinese are trained to write with their right hands[   ] for it is difficult to do Chinese calligraphy with the left hand.   9. _____

10. Before you meet clients for the first time[   ] learn all that you can about their company, their style, and their risk-taking ability.   10. _____

11. He sat down at his desk last evening[   ] and made a preliminary draft of his speech.   11. _____

12. Julie went into the library[   ] but she hurried out a few minutes later.   12. _____

13. Lincoln spoke eloquently about government of the people[   ] by the people[   ] and for the people.   13. _____

14. After she had listened to her favorite album[   ] she settled down to study.   14. _____

15. The candidate gave a number of speeches in Illinois[   ] where she hoped to win support.   15. _____

16. She had always wanted to visit the small village[   ] where her father lived, but she knew neither its name nor its location.   16. _____

17. My instructor[   ] Dr. Ursula Tyler[   ] outlined the work for the current semester.   17. _____

18. What you need[   ] David[   ] is a professional organizer to straighten out your office.   18. _____

independent clauses joined by
    conjunction (**ind**)
introductory adverb clause (**intro**)
series (**ser**)
parenthetical expression (**par**)
nonrestrictive clause (**nr**)

appositive (**app**)
absolute phrase (**abs**)
direct address (**add**)
mild interjection (**inter**)
direct quotation (**quot**)

19. "Is this[   ]" she asked[   ] "the only excuse that you have to offer?"   19. _____

20. Castles were cold and filthy[   ] according to historians[   ] because castles were built more
    for protection than convenience.   20. _____

21. His hands swollen from five fire-ant bites[   ] John swore that he would rid his yard of all
    ant hills.   21. _____

22. Both potato and corn crops had a major impact on the life expectancy of Europeans[   ]
    living in the eighteenth century.   22. _____

23. Ford's first Model T sold for $850 in 1908[   ] but the price dropped to $440 in 1915 because
    of mass production.   23. _____

24. We were asked to read *The Grapes of Wrath*[   ] which John Steinbeck wrote in the 1930s.   24. _____

25. Lorraine Hansberry[   ] the author of *A Raisin in the Sun*[   ] died at age thirty-five.   25. _____

Part 2

If **no comma** is needed in the bracketed space(s), leave the blank empty. If **one or more commas** are needed,
write in the **reason** from the list below (only one reason per blank; use the abbreviations in parentheses).

parenthetical expression (**par**)
after yes and no (**y/n**)
examples introduced by *such as*,
    especially, or *particularly* (**examp**)
contrast (**cont**)
nonrestrictive clause (**nr**)

omission (**om**)
confirmatory question (**ques**)
direct address (**add**)
date (**date**)
state or country (**s/c**)

Examples: He came from New York; she[   ] from Maine.   ____om____
          The Secretary of State[   ] held a press conference.
                                                                                                 _____

1. On New York's number 7 subway line[   ] which runs through Queens[   ] one can hear more
   languages spoken than almost anywhere in the world.   1. _____

2. Senator[   ] would you comment on reports that you will not run again?   2. _____

3. Menlo Park[   ] New Jersey[   ] was Edison's home.   3. _____

4. Seashells are an exquisite natural sculpture[   ] aren't they?   4. _____

5. The decision to have the surgery[   ] of course[   ] should be based on several doctors' opinions. 5. _____

6. Clarissa Denton[   ] who wrote that note to you[   ] needs a lesson in manners!   6. _____

7. The person[   ] who wrote that note to you[   ] needs a lesson in manners!   7. _____

8. For this production, John played Robert; Judith[   ] Harriet.   8. _____

9. Is it true[   ] sir[   ] that you are unwilling to be interviewed by the press?   9. _____

10. Marisa Martinez came all the way from San Antonio[   ] Texas[   ] to attend college in Cleveland. 10. _____

parenthetical expression (**par**)   omission (**om**)
after yes and no (**y/n**)   confirmatory question (**ques**)
examples introduced by *such as*,   direct address (**add**)
   especially, or *particularly* (**examp**)   date (**date**)
contrast (**cont**)   state or country (**s/c**)
nonrestrictive clause (**nr**)

---

11. Frank graduated from the University of Michigan; Esther[ ] from Columbia University.

11. _____

12. Students[ ] who work their way through college[ ] learn to value their college training.

12. _____

13. She said, "No[ ] I absolutely refuse to answer your question."

13. _____

14. Latin America has many types of terrain[ ] such as lowlands, rain forests, vast plains, high plateaus, and fertile valleys.

14. _____

15. On September 11[ ] 2001[ ] people throughout the world were horrified by what they saw on television.

15. _____

16. The film had been advertised as a children's picture[ ] not a production full of violence.

16. _____

17. We were fortunate[ ] nevertheless[ ] to have recovered all of our luggage.

17. _____

18. The average person in the Middle Ages never owned a book[ ] or even saw one.

18. _____

19. You will join us at the art museum[ ] won't you?

19. _____

20. I've already told you[ ] little boy[ ] that I'm not giving back your ball.

20. _____

21. Ralph Ellison[ ] who wrote *Invisible Man*[ ] is also well known for his essays, interviews, and speeches.

21. _____

22. Not everyone[ ] who objected to the new ruling[ ] signed the petition.

22. _____

23. It was[ ] on the other hand[ ] an opportunity that he could not turn down.

23. _____

24. William Clinton[ ] who was our forty-second President[ ] was only the third to face impeachment hearings.

24. _____

25. She enjoys several hobbies[ ] especially collecting coins and writing verse.

25. _____

44. PUNCTUATION: The Comma

(Study 201–203, The Comma)

Part 1

If **no comma** is needed in the bracketed space(s), leave the blank empty. If **one or more commas** are needed, write in the **reason** from the list below (only one reason per blank; use the abbreviations in parentheses).

independent clauses joined by
   conjunction (**ind**)
introductory clause or phrase(s) (**intro**)
series (**ser**)
contrast (**cont**)

appositive (**app**)
absolute phrase (**abs**)
coordinate adjectives (**adj**)
mild interjection (**inter**)
direct quotation (**quot**)

Examples: The New England states include Vermont[ ] Maine[ ] and New Hampshire.   _____ser_____
    The Secretary of State[ ] held a press conference.   _____

1. In India one can be treated for mental illness in a hospital[ ] or at a healing temple.   1._____

2. Oh[ ] don't worry about the traffic at this time of day.   2._____

3. Ernest Hemingway[ ] a distinctive stylist[ ] endured countless parodies of his writing.   3._____

4. Confused by the jumble of direction signs at the intersection[ ] Lomanto pulled into a gas station to ask for help.   4._____

5. The concert having ended[ ] the fans rushed toward the stage.   5._____

6. He hoped to write short stories[ ] publish his poems[ ] and plan a novel.   6._____

7. If the fog continues[ ] we'll have to postpone our trip.   7._____

8. Many people had tried to reach the top of the mountain[ ] yet only a few had succeeded.   8._____

9. Equipped with only an inexpensive camera[ ] she succeeded in taking a prize-winning picture.   9._____

10. During times of emotional distress and heightened tensions[ ] Lee remains calm.   10._____

11. To prepare for her finals[ ] Cathy studied in the library all week.   11._____

12. Recognizing that his position was hopeless[ ] James resigned.   12._____

13. Airbags in cars have saved many lives during crashes[ ] but they can be dangerous for children under twelve.   13._____

14. Mr. Novak found himself surrounded by noisy[ ] exuberant students.   14._____

15. "We are[ ]" she said[ ] "prepared to serve meals to a group of considerable size."   15._____

16. The study found that the experimental medication did not significantly reduce blood pressure[ ] nor did it lower patients' heart rates.   16._____

17. To improve a child's diet[ ] add more beans and green vegetables to the meal.   17._____

18. Although Derek was an excellent driver[ ] he still had difficulty finding a sponsor for the race.   18._____

19. "You must be more quiet[ ] or the landlord will make us move," she said.   19._____

20. Dave Smithers[   ] the sophomore class president[   ] campaigned for an increase in campus activities.

20. _____

21. I could not decide whether to attend college[   ] or to travel to Nigeria with my aunt.

21. _____

22. Built on a high cliff[   ] the house afforded a panoramic view of the valley below.

22. _____

23. Our phone constantly ringing[   ] we decided to rely on the answering machine to avoid interruptions during supper.

23. _____

24. The professor raised his voice to a low roar[   ] the class having apparently dozed off.

24. _____

25. Her courses included Russian[   ] organic chemistry[   ] and marine biology.

25. _____

Part 2

Write **C** if the punctuation in brackets is **correct**.
Write **X** if it is **incorrect**.
(Use only one letter for each answer.)

Example: The New England states include Vermont[,] Maine[,] and New Hampshire.

_____C_____

1. All the art classes visited the Museum of Modern Art[,] when it held its long-awaited Matisse retrospective.

1. _____

2. We traveled to Idaho[,] and went down the Snake River.

2. _____

3. "The records show," the clerk declared[,] "that there is a balance due of $38.76."

3. _____

4. As they trudged deeper into the woods[,] they recalled legends of the Great Brown Bear and began to look around warily.

4. _____

5. You expect to graduate in June[,] don't you?

5. _____

6. O'Connor started the second half at linebacker[,] Bryant having torn his knee ligaments.

6. _____

7. O'Connor started the second half at linebacker[,] Bryant had torn his knee ligaments.

7. _____

8. Trying to concentrate[,] Susan closed the door and turned off the television set.

8. _____

9. "My fellow Americans[,] I look forward to the opportunity to serve this country," he said.

9. _____

10. The newly elected President, on the eve of his inauguration, declared[,] "Saving Social Security and Medicare will receive priority in my administration."

10. _____

11. Helen, who especially enjoys baseball, sat in the front row[,] and watched the game closely.

11. _____

12. "Are you going to a fire?"[,] the police officer asked the speeding motorist.

12. _____

13. Two of the students left the office[,] the third waited to see the dean.

13. _____

14. Angela and two of her friends[,] recently performed at the student talent show.

14. _____

15. "I won't wait any longer," she said[,] picking up her books from the bench.

15. _____

16. His tough[,] angry attitude was only a way to prevent others from knowing how scared he was about failing.

16. _____

17. The relatively short drought[,] nonetheless[,] had still caused much damage to the crops.

17. _____

18. The apartment they rented[,] had no screens or storm windows.

18. _____

19. According to the polls, the candidate was losing[,] he blamed the media for the results.

19. _____

20. The challenger[,] said the incumbent[,] was a tax evader. [The incumbent was making a statement about the challenger.]

20. _____

21. The challenger[,] said the incumbent[,] was a tax evader. [The challenger was making a statement about the incumbent.]

21. _____

22. "Did you know," the financial aid officer replied[,] "that each year thousands of scholarships go unclaimed?"

22. _____

23. Her English professor[,] who was having difficulty getting to class on time[,] requested that the class move to a different building.

23. _____

24. F. Scott Fitzgerald[,] the author of *The Great Gatsby*[,] grew up in Minnesota.

24. _____

25. Next summer she hopes to fulfill a lifelong wish[,] to travel to Alaska by ship.

25. _____

45. PUNCTUATION: The Comma

(Study 201–203, The Comma)

Part 1

Write **C** if the punctuation in brackets is **correct**.
Write **X** if it is **incorrect**.
(Use only one letter for each blank.)

Example: Since they had no further business there[,] they left.   _____C_____

1. The campaign hit a new low when the candidates began accusing each other of embezzlement[,]
    tax fraud[,] and even marital infidelity.   1. _____

2. Piloting a barge towboat on the Mississippi[,] requires not just skill but a thorough knowledge
    of the river.   2. _____

3. In the haste of the evacuation[,] civilian personnel had to leave most of their valuables behind.   3. _____

4. Having turned on her word processor[,] Colleen began her great American novel.   4. _____

5. Haven't you any idea[,] of the responsibility involved in running a household?   5. _____

6. First-graders now engage in writing journals[,] in problem-solving activities[,] and in brief
    science experiments.   6. _____

7. Shaking hands with his patient, the physician asked[,] "Now what kind of surgery are we
    doing today?"   7. _____

8. Peter's goal was to make a short film in graduate school[,] and not worry about a future career.   8. _____

9. Erron and Nakita determined to find a less painful[,] but effective diet.   9. _____

10. The American cowboys' hats actually had many purposes besides shielding their faces from
    the sun and rain[,] for many cowboys used their hats as pillows and drinking cups.   10. _____

11. During conversations about controversial topics[,] our faces often communicate our thoughts,
    especially our emotional responses.   11. _____

12. Harry Rosen[,] a skilled, polished speaker[,] effectively used humor during his speeches.   12. _____

13. To understand how living arrangements affect student relationships[,] the psychology
    department completed several informal observational studies on campus.   13. _____

14. Many music lovers insist[,] that the now-obsolete vinyl LP record produces better sound quality
    than the currently popular CD.   14. _____

15. The states with the greatest numbers of dairy cows are Wisconsin[,] and California.   15. _____

16. Young Soo's mother was preparing *kimchi*[,] a pickled cabbage dish that is commonly
    eaten with Korean meals.   16. _____

17. Having friends must be an important aspect of our culture[,] for many popular television
    series focus on how a group of characters care for their friendships with one another.   17. _____

18. People beginning an intimate relationship use a significant number of affectionate
    expressions[,] but the frequency of these expressions drops as the relationship matures.   18. _____

19. Working hard to pay the mortgage, to educate their children, and to save money for retirement[,] many of America's middle class now call themselves the "new poor."

19. _____

20. The children could take martial arts classes near home[,] or they could decide to save their money for summer camp.

20. _____

21. Now only 68 percent of American children live with both biological parents[,] 20 percent of children live in single-parent families[,] and 9 percent live with one biological parent and a stepparent.

21. _____

22. Jeff was hungry for a gooey[,] chocolate brownie smothered in whipped cream and chocolate sauce.

22. _____

23. His thoughts dominated by grief[,] Jack decided to postpone his vacation for another month.

23. _____

24. "Oh[,] I forgot to bring my report home to finish it tonight," sighed Mary.

24. _____

25. People exercise because it makes them feel good[,] they may even become addicted to exercise.

25. _____

Part 2

In each sentence the brackets show where a comma may or may not be needed. In the blank, write the **number of commas** needed. If none, write **0**.

Example: Lucy ordered a hamburger[ ] a salad[ ] and a soda[ ] with plenty of ice.
_____2_____

1. In addition to your college application form[ ] you need[ ] an official high school transcript[ ] three letters of recommendation[ ] and a check for the fee.

1. _____

2. Although it is not required[ ] by state law[ ] the presence of a lifeguard would have prevented[ ] the nearly fatal accident.

2. _____

3. According to Robert Darnton's research[ ] the story "Little Red Riding Hood[ ]" may reveal[ ] some information[ ] about the anxieties and issues of eighteenth-century French peasants.

3. _____

4. My fellow Americans[ ] can we allow other nations[ ] who pose as friends[ ] to threaten our security?

4. _____

5. I wanted[ ] to go[ ] to Harvard; Terry[ ] to Yale.

5. _____

6. I[ ] didn't realize[ ] that four Latin American writers[ ] have won the Nobel Prize for Literature.

6. _____

7. Unlike the Maya[ ] and Aztecs[ ] the Incas had no written language[ ] but instead[ ] they kept records on knotted strings called *quipus*.

7. _____

8. The chairman[ ] who had already served two terms in Congress[ ] and one in the State Assembly[ ] declared his candidacy again.

8. _____

9. Jack was born on December 1[ ] 1990[ ] in Fargo[ ] North Dakota[ ] during a blizzard.

9. _____

10. I consider him[ ] to be[ ] a hard-working student, but[ ] I may be wrong.

10. _____

11. Audrey Starke[ ] a woman[ ] whom I met last summer[ ] is here[ ] to see me.

11. _____

12. Having an interest[ ] in anthropology[ ] she frequently audited[ ] Dr. Irwin's class[ ] that met on Saturdays.

12. _____

13. Native Americans were the first to grow corn[ ] potatoes[ ] squash[ ] pumpkins[ ] and avocados.

13. _____

14. Well[ ] I dislike her intensely[ ] but[ ] she is quite clever[ ] to be sure.

14. _____

15. To solve[ ] her legal problems[ ] she consulted an attorney[ ] that she knew[ ] from college.

     15. _____

16. "To what[ ]" he asked[ ] "do you attribute[ ] your great popularity[ ] with the students?"

     16. _____

17. From Native Americans[ ] the world learned about cinnamon[ ] and chocolate[ ] and chicle[ ] the main ingredient in chewing gum.

     17. _____

18. "Blowin' in the Wind[ ]" a folk song written by Bob Dylan[ ] in 1962[ ] promises[ ] that life will get better through time.

     18. _____

19. Many filmmakers are creating[ ] serious movies[ ] about their cultural heritage; however, there are[ ] few commercially successful movies about Asian American cultures.

     19. _____

20. "You haven't seen my glasses[ ] have you?" Granny asked[ ] the twins[ ] thinking they had hidden them[ ] somewhere in the living room.

     20. _____

21. The car having broken down[ ] because of a dirty carburetor[ ] we missed the first act[ ] in which[ ] Hamlet confronts his father's ghost.

     21. _____

22. After she had paid her tuition[ ] she checked in at the residence hall[ ] that she had selected[ ] and soon began[ ] unloading her suitcases and boxes.

     22. _____

23. The space launch went so punctually[ ] and smoothly[ ] that the astronauts began their voyage[ ] relaxed[ ] and confident.

     23. _____

24. Chinese porcelain[ ] which is prized for its beauty[ ] and its translucence[ ] was copied[ ] by seventeenth-century Dutch potters.

     24. _____

25. The road to Brattleboro[ ] being coated with ice[ ] we proceeded[ ] slowly[ ] and cautiously.

     25. _____

46. PUNCTUATION: The Comma

(Study 201–203, The Comma)

Part 1

Either **insert** or **cross out a comma** to make the sentence correct. In the blank, write the word that comes just **before** the inserted or crossed-out comma.

Examples: When the soldiers looked around, the stranger had vanished.   ___around___

The cloud-hidden sun⟋ gave us no clue as to which way was south.   ___sun___

1. They could have followed the state highway to the right but they chose the local road to the left.   1. _____

2. The 1990s will be remembered by most Americans, as a decade of rising prosperity.   2. _____

3. Having examined and reexamined the ancient manuscript the committee of scholars declared it genuine.   3. _____

4. If the weather is pleasant and dry, we will march in the St. Patrick's Day parade, and then dance at a parish party.   4. _____

5. Amanda has decided to write a cookbook, remodel her kitchen and travel through California.   5. _____

6. Many Americans now prefer news sources, that offer human interest stories.   6. _____

7. The country, that receives the most media attention often is the recipient of the most aid from the United Nations.   7. _____

8. Coaching soccer, and teaching part-time at a local college keep me quite busy.   8. _____

9. George and Robert thoroughly and painstakingly considered, what had to be done to defuse the bomb.   9. _____

10. If ever there was the law on one side, and simple justice on the other, here is such a situation.   10. _____

11. Ann Tyler, who won a Pulitzer Prize in 1988 has recently written a novel about a woman in her forties who runs away from her family.   11. _____

12. Hillary Clinton, will be remembered as the first First Lady to gain an elective office of her own.   12. _____

13. Claiming that he was just offering good advice Ace frequently would tell me which card to play.   13. _____

14. What gave Helen the inspiration for her short story, was her mother's account of growing up on a farm.   14. _____

15. Owen's baseball cards included such famous examples as Willie Mays's running catch in the 1954 World Series, and Hank Aaron's record-breaking home run.   15. _____

16. The volume that was the most valuable in the library's rare book collection, was a First Folio edition of Shakespeare's plays.   16. _____

17. *Gone with the Wind*, a film enjoyed by millions of people throughout the world was first thought unlikely to be a commercial success.   17. _____

18. Because the material was difficult to understand Monica decided to hire a tutor.   18. _____

19. The study asserted that parents in sending their infant children to day care, may be slowing their youngsters' mental development.

19. _____

20. Although everyone was ready for the test no one complained when Professor Smith canceled it.

20. _____

Part 2

Write an original sentence that contains an example of the comma used as stated in the brackets. **Circle** the comma(s) so used.

_____

Example: [Setting off a parenthetical expression] <u>This course, it seems to me, requires too much work.</u>

(Collaborative option: Students work in pairs or small groups to suggest and comment on different examples.)

1. [between two independent clauses] _____

_____

_____

2. [with an introductory adverb clause] _____

_____

_____

3. [with coordinate adjectives] _____

_____

_____

4. [with a long introductory prepositional phrase or a series of introductory prepositional phrases or an introductory verbal phrase] _____

_____

_____

5. [with an absolute phrase] _____

_____

_____

6. [with a parenthetical expression] _____

_____

_____

7. [with an expression of contrast] _____

_____

_____

8. [with a date or address] _____

_____

_____

9. [with a nonrestrictive clause or phrase] _____

_____

_____

10. [with a direct quotation] _____

_____

_____

11. [to prevent misreading] _____

_____

_____

12. [in direct address] _____

_____

_____

13. [Write a sentence with a *restrictive* clause—one that does **not** use commas.] _____

_____

_____

47. PUNCTUATION: The Period, Question Mark, and Exclamation Point

(Study 204–205, The Period; 206–207, The Question Mark; and 208–209, The Exclamation Point)

Write **C** if the punctuation in brackets is **correct**.
Write **X** if it is **incorrect**.

Example: Is there any word from the Awards Committee yet[?]   _____C_____

1. The judge would never hold me in contempt, would she[?]   1. _____
2. "Move back; the fire's advancing!" shouted the forest ranger[!]   2. _____
3. The police officer calmly inquired whether I had the slightest notion of just how fast I was backing up[?]   3. _____
4. Mr. Hall and Miss[.] James will chair the committee.   4. _____
5. The chem[.] test promises to be challenging.   5. _____
6. Where is the office? Down the hall on the left[.]   6. _____
7. Good afternoon, ma'am[.] May I present you with a free scrub brush?   7. _____
8. "How much did the owners spend on players' salaries?" the reporter asked[?]   8. _____
9. His next question—wouldn't you know[?]—was, "What do you need, ma'am?"   9. _____
10. "Wow! Does your computer have a video camera too[!]"   10. _____
11. "What a magnificent view you have of the mountains[!]" said he.   11. _____
12. Who said, "If at first you don't succeed, try, try again" [?]   12. _____
13. Would you please check my computer for viruses[?]   13. _____
14. HELP WANTED: Editor[.] for our new brochure.   14. _____
15. Pat, please type this memo[.] to the purchasing department.   15. _____
16. What? You lent that scoundrel Snively $10,000[?!]   16. _____
17. I asked her why, of all the men on campus, she had chosen him[?]   17. _____
18. Why did I do it? Because I respected her[.] Jackie worked hard to finish her degree.   18. _____
19. "Footloose and Fancy Free[.]" [title of an essay]   19. _____
20. Would you please send me your reply by e-mail[.]   20. _____
21. "The Lakers win[!!]" the announcer screamed as Bryant's jump shot slipped through the net at the buzzer.   21. _____
22. Charlie was an inspiring [(?)] date. He burped all through dinner.   22. _____
23. My supervisor asked how much equipment I would need to update the computer center[.]   23. _____
24. The essay was "Computers: Can We Live Without Them[?]"   24. _____
25. I heard the news on station W[.]I[.]N[.]K.   25. _____
26. The postmark on the package read "Springfield, MA[.] 01102."   26. _____
27. The monarch who followed King George VI[.] was Queen Elizabeth II.   27. _____

28. According to Ramsey, "The election drew a light turnout[.] . . . Predictably, the Socialist Party won."

28. _____

29. You lost your wallet again[?] I don't believe it.

29. _____

30. The duke was born in 1576[(?)] and died in 1642.

30. _____

31. What[!?] What did you just call me?

31. _____

32. Do you know when I may expect my refund[?]

32. _____

33. Could I have committed the crime? Never[.] I was on a business trip to St. Louis at the time.

33. _____

48. PUNCTUATION: The Semicolon

(Study 210, The Semicolon)

Part 1

Write the **reason** for the semicolon in each sentence (use the abbreviations in parentheses). Use only one reason for each sentence.

between clauses lacking a coordinating conjunction (**no conj**)
between clauses joined by a conjunctive adverb (**conj adv**)
between clauses having commas within them (**cl w com**)
in a series having commas within the items (**ser w com**)

Example: It was a glorious day for the North; it was a sad one for the South.   <u>no conj</u>

1. Pressure-treated wood has been popular for decks because it resists the elements for years; however, its arsenic content has made it environmentally undesirable.   1. _____

2. The farmers are using an improved fertilizer; thus their crop yields have increased.   2. _____

3. Still to come were Perry, a trained squirrel; Arnold, an acrobat; and Mavis, a magician.   3. _____

4. "Negotiations," he said, "have collapsed; we will strike at noon."   4. _____

5. Tacoma's Museum of Glass is one of only two museums in the country dedicated to exhibiting glass; the other is the Corning Museum of Glass in upstate New York.   5. _____

6. The average Internet user spends about six hours a week online; the majority of these users reach the Internet from work.   6. _____

7. Pam, who lives in the suburbs, drives her car to work each day; yet Ruben, her next-door neighbor, takes the bus.   7. _____

8. Changing your time-management habits requires determination; therefore, begin by writing down your goals.   8. _____

9. The play was performed in Altoona, Pennsylvania; Buckhannon, West Virginia; and The Woodlands, Texas.   9. _____

10. Flight 330 stops at Little Rock, Dallas, and Albuquerque; but Flight 440, the all-coach special, is an express to Phoenix.   10. _____

Part 2

If a **semicolon is needed** in the brackets, write the **reason** in the blank, as you did in part 1 (**no conj, conj adv, cl w com, ser w com**). If **no semicolon** is needed, leave the blank empty.

Examples: He would not help her get the job[ ] moreover, he could not.   <u>conj adv</u>
         After the rap concert[ ] we drove to Salty's.   _____

1. The Puritans banned the Christmas holiday when they settled in North America[ ] the holiday was not revived until the 1880s.   1. _____

2. Shall I telephone to find out the time[ ] when the box office opens?   2. _____

between clauses lacking a coordinating conjunction (**no conj**)
between clauses joined by a conjunctive adverb (**conj adv**)
between clauses having commas within them (**cl w com**)
in a series having commas within the items (**ser w com**)

3. A recent study indicates that saccharin does not cause cancer in humans[ ] the only consumers who should worry are laboratory rats.

3. _____

4. The lake suffered from a buildup of stream-borne silt[ ] until it became so shallow that it had to be dredged.

4. _____

5. The lake suffered from a buildup of stream-borne silt[ ] it became so shallow that it had to be dredged.

5. _____

6. The surprises in the team's starting lineup were Garcia, the second baseman[ ] Hudler, the shortstop[ ] and Fitzgerald, the catcher.

6. _____

7. The national public education system needs to redefine its expectations[ ] because most schools do not expect all of their students to succeed.

7. _____

8. Hollywood has always portrayed the Union soldiers as dressed in blue and the Confederate troops in gray[ ] however, for the first year of the Civil War, most soldiers wore their state militia uniforms, which came in many colors.

8. _____

9. Soft drinks are a traditional beverage in the United States[ ] flavored soda water first appeared in 1825 in Philadelphia.

9. _____

10. Orville and Wilbur Wright ran a bicycle shop in Dayton, had no scientific training, and never finished high school[ ] yet, by inventing the airplane, they revolutionized transportation worldwide.

10. _____

11. She is very bright[ ] at twenty, she is the owner of a successful small business.

11. _____

12. John uses a video conferencing network to conduct business[ ] instead of spending time flying all over the world for meetings.

12. _____

13. Exercising is quite beneficial[ ] because it helps to reduce physical and psychological stress.

13. _____

14. Our representatives included Will Leeds, a member of the Rotary Club[ ] Augusta Allcott, a banker[ ] and Bill Rogers, president of the Chamber of Commerce.

14. _____

15. Peter lives in Minnesota[ ] Howard, in Maryland.

15. _____

49. PUNCTUATION: The Semicolon and the Comma

(Study 201–203, The Comma, and 210, The Semicolon)

Write **com** if you would insert a **comma** (or commas) in the brackets.
Write **semi** if you would insert a **semicolon** (or semicolons).
If you would insert nothing, leave the blank empty.
Write only one answer for each blank.

Example: The milk had all gone sour[ ] we could not have our cappucino.   ____semi____

1. The flood waters rose steadily throughout the night[ ] by dawn our kitchen was flooded to the countertops.   1. _____

2. Many Americans have financial plans for retirement[ ] but stock-market turmoil has made them rethink those plans.   2. _____

3. Dr. Jones[ ] who teaches geology[ ] graduated from MIT.   3. _____

4. The Dr. Jones[ ] who teaches geology[ ] graduated from MIT.   4. _____

5. I met the woman[ ] who is to be president of the new junior college.   5. _____

6. She likes working in Washington, D.C.[ ] she hopes to remain there permanently.   6. _____

7. To the east we could see the White Mountains[ ] to the west, the Green.   7. _____

8. Read the article carefully[ ] then write an essay on the author's handling of the subject.   8. _____

9. One of my grandmother's most prized possessions is an antique glass bowl[ ] that was made in Murano, Italy.   9. _____

10. The game being beyond our reach[ ] the coach told me to start warming up.   10. _____

11. We're going on a cruise around the bay on Sunday[ ] and we'd like you to come with us.   11. _____

12. If Amy decides to become a lawyer[ ] you can be sure she'll be a good one.   12. _____

13. Customer satisfaction is important[ ] the owners, therefore, hired a consulting firm to conduct a customer survey.   13. _____

14. Li-Young registered for an advanced biology course[ ] otherwise, she might not have been admitted to medical school.   14. _____

15. The newest computers[ ] moreover[ ] are cheaper than last year's less powerful models.   15. _____

16. Cell phones are rapidly gaining in popularity[ ] but these phones do not work from some remote areas.   16. _____

17. He began his speech again[ ] fire engines having drowned out his opening remarks.   17. _____

18. The best day of the vacation occurred[ ] when we took the children sledding.   18. _____

19. Let me introduce the new officers: Phillip Whitaker, president[ ] Elaine Donatelli, secretary[ ] and Pierre Northrup, treasurer.   19. _____

20. We thought of every possible detail when planning the dinner party[ ] yet we didn't anticipate our cat's jumping into the cake.   20. _____

21. We have known the Floyd Archers[ ] ever since they moved here from New Jersey.   21. _____

22. The actor Hal Holbrook has successfully portrayed Mark Twain[ ] everywhere in the country for more than forty years.   22. _____

23. The drama coach was a serene person[ ] not one to be worried about nervous amateurs.   23. _____

24. To turn them into professional performers was[ ] needless to say[ ] an impossible task.   24. _____

25. "Yes, I will attend the review session," Jack said[ ] "if you can guarantee that the time spent will be worthwhile."   25. _____

26. Call the security office[ ] if there seems to be any problem with the locks.   26. _____

27. Couples with severe disabilities may have difficulty raising a family[ ] there are few programs to help disabled parents with their children.   27. _____

28. Britain was the first Common Market country to react[ ] others quickly followed suit.   28. _____

29. The American troops stormed ashore at Omaha and Utah beaches[ ] the British, at Sword, Gold, and Juno.   29. _____

30. Perhaps because the weather was finally warm again[ ] I didn't want to stay inside.   30. _____

31. American couples are examining their lifestyles[ ] many are cutting back in their work schedules to spend more time with their children.   31. _____

32. The World Series hadn't yet begun[ ] however, he had equipped himself with a new radio.   32. _____

33. I could not remember ever having seen her as radiantly happy[ ] as she now was.   33. _____

34. No, I cannot go to the game[ ] I have a term paper to finish.   34. _____

35. Kristi Yamaguchi[ ] in fact, is a fourth-generation Japanese American.   35. _____

36. Victor, on the other hand[ ] played the best game of his career.   36. _____

37. Home-grown products are common in rural farming communities[ ] on the other hand, such products can command high prices in urban areas.   37. _____

38. "There will be no rain today[ ]" she insisted. "The weather forecaster says so."   38. _____

39. Swimming is an excellent form of exercise[ ] swimming for twenty-six minutes consumes 100 calories.   39. _____

40. Though the American flag had only forty-eight stars in 1944[ ] the war movie mistakenly showed a fifty-star flag.   40. _____

41. The short story[ ] that impressed me the most[ ] was written by a thirty-five-year-old police officer.   41. _____

42. Mary constantly counts calories and fat content in the food she eats[ ] yet she never loses more than a pound.   42. _____

43. Many cultures follow different calendars[ ] for example, the Jewish New Year is celebrated in the fall, the Vietnamese and Chinese New Year at the beginning of the year, and the Cambodian New Year in April.   43. _____

44. "My fraternity[ ]" stated Travis, "completes numerous community service projects throughout the school year."   44. _____

45. All the students were present for the final, but[ ] most were suffering from the flu.   45. _____

46. Muslim students on campus asked the administration for a larger international student center[ ] and a quiet place for their daily prayers.   46. _____

47. Whenever Sam is feeling sad and discouraged about his job[ ] he puts on a Tony Bennett record and dances with the dog.   47. _____

48. Barry and I were planning a large farewell party for Eugene within the next month[ ] but certainly not next week.   48. _____

49. To read only mysteries and novels[ ] was my plan for the holiday break.   49. _____

50. Most Amish reside in Pennsylvania[ ] however, there are settlements also in Ohio and upstate New York.   50. _____

50. PUNCTUATION: The Semicolon and the Comma

(Study 201–203, The Comma, and 210, The Semicolon)

Write an **original sentence** illustrating the use of the semicolon or comma stated in brackets.

_____

Example: [two independent clauses with no coordinating conjunction between them]
<u>Five students scored A on the exam; four scored D.</u>

(Collaborative option: Students work in pairs or small groups to suggest and comment on different examples.)

1. [two independent clauses with *furthermore* between them] _____

   _____

   _____

2. [two independent clauses joined by *and*, with commas within the clauses] _____

   _____

   _____

3. [two independent clauses joined by *yet*] _____

   _____

   _____

4. [three items in a series, with commas within each of the items] _____

   _____

   _____

5. [two independent clauses with *then* between them] _____

   _____

   _____

6. [two independent clauses with no word between them] _____

   _____

   _____

7. [an introductory adverb clause] _____

   _____

   _____

8. [a nonrestrictive clause] _____

   _____

   _____

9. [two independent clauses with *in fact* or *also* between them]_____

   _____

   _____

10. [two independent clauses with *however* inside the second clause (not between the clauses)] _____

    _____

    _____

51. PUNCTUATION: The Apostrophe

(Study 211–213, The Apostrophe)

In the first blank, write the number of the **correct** choice (**1** or **2**). In the second blank, write the **reason** for your choice (use the abbreviations in parentheses; if your choice for the first blank has no apostrophe, leave the second blank empty).

singular possessive (**sing pos**)   contraction (**cont**)
plural possessive (**pl pos**)   plural of letter or symbol used as a word (**let/sym**)

Examples: The fault was (1) **Jacob's** (2) **Jacobs'**.   <u>1</u>   sing pos
          The fault was (1) **your's** (2) **yours**.   <u>2</u>   _____

1. It (1)**wasn't** (2)**was'nt** the weather that caused the delay; it was an electrical failure.   1. ____ _____

2. The (1)**Smith's** (2)**Smiths** have planned a murder-mystery party.   2. ____ _____

3. The (1)**James'** (2)**Jameses** are moving to Seattle.   3. ____ _____

4. My (1)**brother-in-law's** (2)**brother's-in-law** medical practice is flourishing.   4. ____ _____

5. The (1)**Novotny's** (2)**Novotnys'** new home is spacious.   5. ____ _____

6. (1)**Its** (2)**It's** important to exercise several times a week.   6. ____ _____

7. (1)**Who's** (2)**Whose** responsible for the increased production of family-oriented movies?   7. ____ _____

8. The two (1)**girl's** (2)**girls'** talent was quite evident to everyone.   8. ____ _____

9. Some economists fear that the Social Security system may be bankrupt by the (1)**2020s** (2)**2020's**.   9. ____ _____

10. It will be a two-(1)**day's** (2)**days'** drive to Galveston.   10. ____ _____

11. The dispute over the last clause caused a (1)**weeks** (2)**week's** delay in the contract signing.   11. ____ _____

12. Mary accidentally spilled tea on her (1)**bosses** (2)**boss's** report.   12. ____ _____

13. After the long absence, they fell into (1)**each others'** (2)**each other's** arms.   13. ____ _____

14. Each woman claimed that the diamond ring was (1)**her's** (2)**hers**.   14. ____ _____

15. Geraldine uses too many (1)*and*s (2)*and*'s in most of her presentations.   15. ____ _____

16. Bumstead never dots his (1)**I's** (2)**Is**.   16. ____ _____

17. (1)**Wer'ent** (2)**Weren't** you surprised by the success of her book?   17. ____ _____

18. Which is safer, your van or (1)**ours** (2)**our's**?   18. ____ _____

19. Georgiana insisted, "I (1)**have'nt** (2)**haven't** seen Sandy for weeks."   19. ____ _____

20. He bought fifty (1)**cents** (2)**cents'** worth of bubblegum.   20. ____ _____

21. The back alley was known to be a (1)**thieve's** (2)**thieves'** hangout.   21. ____ _____

22. (1)**Paul's and David's** (2)**Paul and David's** senior project was praised by their advisor.   22. ____ _____

23. The (1)**children's** (2)**childrens'** kitten ate our goldfish.   23. ____ _____

24. "The (1)**evenings** (2)**evening's** been delightful," Lily said. "Thank you."   24. ____ _____

25. The local (1)**coal miner's** (2)**coal miners'** union was the subject of Bill's documentary.   25. ____ _____

52. PUNCTUATION: The Apostrophe

(Study 211–213, The Apostrophe)

For each bracketed apostrophe, write **C** if it is **correct**; write **X** if it is **incorrect**. Use the first column for the first apostrophe, the second column for the second apostrophe.

		C	X
Example: Who[']s on first? Where is todays['] lineup?			
1. Everyone else[']s opinion carries less weight with me than your[']s.	1.		
2. Mrs. Jackson[']s invitation to the William[']s must have gone astray.	2.		
3. He would[']nt know that information after only two day[']s employment.	3.		
4. Were[']nt they fortunate that the stolen car wasn't their[']s?	4.		
5. It[']s a pity that the one bad cabin would be our[']s.	5.		
6. We[']re expecting the Wagner[']s to meet us in Colorado for a ski trip.	6.		
7. Home-baked pizza[']s need an oven temperature in the upper 400[']s.	7.		
8. Does[']nt the governor see that most voters won[']t support her cuts in farm aid?	8.		
9. The two sisters had agreed that they[']d stop wearing each others['] shoes.	9.		
10. She[']s not going to accept anybody[']s advice, no matter how sound it might be.	10.		
11. The three students['] complaints about the professor[']s attitude in class were finally addressed by the administration.	11.		
12. He[']s hoping for ten hours['] work a week in the library.	12.		
13. The idea of a cultural greeting card business was not our[']s; it was Lois[']s.	13.		
14. There are three *i*[']s in the word *optimistic;* there are two *r*[']s in the word *embarrass.*	14.		
15. The computer printout consisted of a series of *1*[']s and *0*[']s.	15.		
16. Their advisor sent two dozen yellow rose[']s to the Women Student Association[']s meeting.	16.		
17. I really did[']nt expect to see all of the drivers['] finish the race.	17.		
18. Hav[']ent you heard about the theft at the Jone[']s house?	18.		
19. The popular mens['] store, established in 1923, was[']nt able to compete with the large discount stores in the nearby mall.	19.		
20. I'm sure that, if he[']s physically able, he[']ll be at the volunteer program.	20.		
21. The responsibility for notifying club members is her[']s, not our[']s.	21.		
22. Can[']t I persuade you that you[']re now ready to move out of the house?	22.		
23. Both lawyers['] used hard-hitting tactic[']s to explain why their company should not be required to pay damages.	23.		
24. Everyones['] agreeing that in the 1990[']s too many stocks were overvalued.	24.		
25. Marie Stockton sought her sister-in-law[']s advice when she considered opening a women[']s fitness salon.	25.		

53. PUNCTUATION: The Apostrophe

(Study 211–213, The Apostrophe)

In the paragraphs below, most words ending in **s** are followed by a small number. At the right are blanks with corresponding numbers. In each blank, write the **correct ending** for the word with that number: **'s** or **s'** or **s**.

Example: We collected our days[51] pay after cleaning the tables[52].

51. _'s_   52. _s_

All young performers[1] dream of gaining recognition from their audiences[2] and of seeing their names in lights[3] on Broadway. These were Annie Smiths[4] dreams when she left her parents[5] home and ran off to New York City. At age eighteen, however, Annie was not prepared for the difficulties[6] of living alone and working in a large city. Her wages[7] as a waitress barely covered a months[8] rent. And she still needed to buy groceries[9] and pay her utilities[10]. It took Annie several months[11] time to find two suitable roommates, who would share the rent and other bills. However, the roommates[12] also helped in other important ways, for when Annie felt that she couldn't go for another audition, her roommates[13] encouragement to continue helped bolster Annies[14] determination. Annie realized that for anyones[15] dream to happen, a great deal of hard work had to come first.

One evening in the late 1990s[16], as she was clearing away the last two customers[17] dishes at Carusos[18] Restaurant, she heard a distinguished-looking woman asking the head waiter, "Whos[19] that young lady? She moves[20] with such grace, and shes[21] got the poise and features[22] of a movie star; I'm a film director, and I'd like to speak to her."

This storys[23] ending is a happy one, for in a years[24] time Annie became a star. All that she had dreamed of was now hers[25].

1.____   2.____
3.____   4.____
5.____
6.____   7.____
8.____   9.____   10.____
11.____
12.____
13.____
14.____   15.____
16.____   17.____
18.____
19.____   20.____   21.____
22.____
23.____   24.____
25.____

54. PUNCTUATION: Italics

(Study 214, Italics [Underlining])

Part 1

Write the **reason** for each use of italics (use the abbreviations in parentheses):

title of printed, performed, or electronic work (**title**)
name of ship, train, plane, or spacecraft (**craft**)
title of painting or sculpture (**art**)
foreign word not Anglicized (**for**)
word, letter, symbol, or figure referred to as such (**wlsf**)
emphasis (**emph**)

Example: Does this library subscribe to
Smithsonian?   __title__

1. The *Andrea Doria* sank after a collision
   with the *Stockholm*.   1. _____

2. Channel 8 seems to show nothing but reruns
   of *Raymond* and *Seinfeld*.   2. _____

3. For many years, the *Manchester Guardian*
   has been a leading newspaper in England.   3. _____

4. Norman Rockwell painted *The Four
   Freedoms* during World War II.   4. _____

5. The directions on the test indicated that all
   questions were to be answered with *1*s or *2*s. 5. _____

6. Dozens of English words connected with dining
   come from the French—*cuisine, à la mode,*
   and *hors d'oeuvres,* to name just a few.   6. _____

7. Susan learned to spell the word *villain* by
   thinking of a "villa in" Italy.   7. _____

8. "Are you sure you won't *ever* cheat on me?"
   she asked.   8. _____

9. The statue *The Women of Belfast* is on loan
   from the Ulster Museum.   9. _____

10. An article had been written recently about
    the submarine *Nautilus*.   10. _____

11. N. Scott Momaday's *1969: The Way to
    Rainy Mountain* recounts the Kiowa
    Indians' migration to the American plains. 11. _____

12. How many *s*'s and *i*'s are there in your
    last name?   12. _____

13. Though *Oklahoma!* was first performed more
    than sixty years ago, it is still a favorite of
    local theater groups.   13. _____

14. The American pronunciation of *vase* is *vayss*
    or *vaze*; the British pronunciation is *vahz*. 14. _____

15. Richard Rodriguez's autobiography, *Hunger
    of Memory*, helped me understand some of
    the issues surrounding bilingual education. 15. _____

16. American women are learning to say a strong
    no to many professional demands so that
    they have time for family and friends.   16. _____

17. Aboard the *Enterprise*, the captain made
    plans to return to the planet Zircon to
    rescue Mr. Spock.   17. _____

18. Michelangelo's *David* was originally mounted
    outdoors but was moved into a museum to
    protect the stone from erosion.   18. _____

19. Now that I have *Ace Anti-virus Protector*
    software installed on my hard drive, I have
    no worries about computer viruses.   19. _____

20. The first American to orbit the earth was
    John Glenn in *Friendship 7*.   20. _____

21. Her printed *R*'s and *B*'s closely resemble
    each other.   21. _____

22. Although he never held office, Lopez was
    the *de facto* ruler of his country.   22. _____

23. Some people spell and pronounce the words
    athlete and *athletics* as if there were an *e*
    after *th* in each word.   23. _____

24. The movie *A Family Thing* addresses racial
    issues in the United States in a thought-
    provoking and sensitive manner.   24. _____

25. The original meaning of the word *mad*
    was "disordered in mind" or "insane."   25. _____

In each sentence, **underline** the word(s) that should be in italics.

___

Example: The cover of <u>Newsweek</u> depicted African refugees.

1. Dave Matthews and his group performed items from their new CD, Busted Stuff.

2. Deciding to come home by ship, we made reservations on the Queen Elizabeth II.

3. Geraldine went downtown to buy copies of Esquire and Field and Stream.

4. "It's time for a change!" shouted the candidate during the debate.

5. Proof, David Auburn's drama about love, fear, genius, and madness, won both the Pulitzer Prize and a Tony Award.

6. The New York Times must have weighed ten pounds last Sunday.

7. The Mystery! series on public television promises amateur sleuths a weekly escape into murder and intrigue.

8. Browsing through recent fiction at the library, Ms. Kovalchik came across The Red Tent, by Anita Diamant.

9. Among the magazines scattered in the room was a copy of Popular Mechanics.

10. Maya Angelou's first published work, I Know Why the Caged Bird Sings, is an autobiography describing her first sixteen years.

11. When I try to pronounce the word statistics, I always stumble over it.

12. I still have difficulty remembering the difference between continual and continuous.

13. "I'll never stop fighting for my rights," Megan Morton thundered. "And I mean never."

14. Picasso's Guernica depicts the horrors of war.

15. The Thinker is a statue that many people admire.

16. Spike Lee's film Malcolm X inspired me.

17. You'll enjoy reading "The Man of the House" in the book Fifty Great Short Stories.

18. The British spelling of the word humor is h-u-m-o-u-r.

19. "How to Heckle Your Prof" was an essay in John James's How to Get Thrown Out of College.

20. Michelangelo's Last Judgment shows "the omnipotence of his artistic ability."

21. The source of the above quotation is the Encyclopaedia Britannica.

22. They were able to download the entire program Master Chess from the Internet.

23. He had been a noted braumeister in Germany.

24. Perry won the spelling bee's award for creative expression with his rendition of antidisestablishmentarianism.

25. The instructor said that Sam's 7s and his 4s look very much alike.

55. PUNCTUATION: Quotation Marks

(Study 215–219, Quotation Marks)

Insert quotation marks at the proper places in each sentence.

Example: She wrote "Best Surfing Beaches" for *Outdoor* magazine.

1. Readers were mesmerized by the article Halle Berry: A True Survivor Story in *Good Housekeeping*.

2. The young couple read the *Better Homes and Gardens* article No Need to Cook.

3. W. C. Fields's dying words were, I'd rather be in Philadelphia.

4. The poem The Swing was written by Robert Louis Stevenson.

5. Be prepared, warned the weather forecaster, for a particularly harsh winter this year.

6. Childhood Memories is a chapter in the reader *Growing Up in the South*.

7. In Kingdom of the Skies, in the magazine *Arizona Highways*, Joyce Muench described the unusual cloud formations that enhance Arizona's scenery.

8. The word *cavalier* was originally defined as a man on a horse.

9. One of the most famous American essays is Emerson's Self-Reliance.

10. One of my favorite short stories is Eudora Welty's A Worn Path.

11. The song The Wind Beneath My Wings was sung to inspire mentors to stay with the literary program.

12. The World Is Too Much with Us is a poem by William Wordsworth.

13. The New Order is an article that appeared in *Time* magazine.

14. An article that appeared in the *Washington Post* is Can We Abolish Poverty?

15. Cousins' essay The Right to Die poses the question of whether suicide is ever an acceptable response to life circumstances.

16. The Love Song of J. Alfred Prufrock is a poem by T. S. Eliot.

17. The dictionary of slang defines *loopy* as slightly crazy.

18. The concluding song of the evening was Auld Lang Syne.

19. We read a poem by Alice Walker entitled Women.

20. Today's local newspaper ran an editorial titled Save the Salmon.

21. What we have here, the burly man said, is a failure to communicate.

22. Never in the field of human combat, said Winston Churchill, has so much been owed by so many to so few.

23. She read Julio Cortazar's short story The Health of the Sick.

24. *Discography* means a comprehensive list of recordings made by a particular performer or of a particular composer's work.

25. How rude of him to say, I don't care to see you!

56. PUNCTUATION: Quotation Marks

(Study 215–219, Quotation Marks)

Write **C** if the punctuation in brackets is **correct**.
Write **X** if it is **not**.

Example: "What time is it["?] wondered Katelyn.   _____X_____

1. The stadium announcer intoned[, "]Ladies and gentlemen, please rise for our national anthem."   1. _____

2. The television interviewer shoved a microphone in the mother's face and demanded, "How did you feel when you heard that your little girl had been kidnapped[?"]   2. _____

3. In the first semester we read Gabriel García Márquez's short story "Big Mama's Funeral[".]   3. _____

4. "Where are you presently employed?[",] the interviewer asked.   4. _____

5. "When you finish your rough draft," said Professor Grill[, "]send it to my e-mail address."   5. _____

6. Who was it who mused, "Where are the snows of yesteryear["?]   6. _____

7. Dr. Nelson, our anthropology teacher, asked, "How many of you have read *The Autobiography of Malcolm X* [?"]   7. _____

8. "We need more study rooms in the library[,"] declared one presidential candidate in the student government debate.   8. _____

9. "Write when you can[,"] Mother said as I left for the airport.   9. _____

10. To *dissuade* means "to persuade someone not to do something[."]   10. _____

11. "Ask not what your country can do for you[;"] ask what you can do for your country."   11. _____

12. He said, "Our language creates problems when we talk about race in America.[" "]We don't have enough terms to explain the complexities of cultural diversity."   12. _____

13. "Do you remember Father's saying, 'Never give up['?"] she asked.   13. _____

14. She began reciting the opening line of one of Elizabeth Barrett Browning's sonnets: "How do I love thee? Let me count the ways[."]   14. _____

15. Gwendolyn Brooks's poem ["]The Bean Eaters["] is one of her best.   15. _____

16. ["]*The Fantasticks,*["] which ran for more than forty years, is the longest-running musical play in American theater.   16. _____

17. "Want to play ball, Scarecrow[?"] the Wicked Witch asked, a ball of fire in her hand.   17. _____

18. "Shall I read aloud Whitman's poem 'Out of the Cradle Endlessly Rocking['?"] she asked.   18. _____

19. Have you read Adrienne Rich's poem "Necessities of Life[?"]   19. _____

20. When Susan saw the show about America's homeless, she exclaimed, "I have to find a way to help[!"]   20. _____

21. The noun *neurotic* is defined as "an emotionally unstable individual[".]   21. _____

22. "I'm going to the newsstand," he said[, "]for a copy of *Sports Illustrated.*"   22. _____

23. "Do you believe in fairies[?"] Peter Pan asks the children.   23. _____

24. How maddening of her to reply calmly, "You're so right["!]   24. _____

25. "I need you in my office right away," the comptroller barked over the phone[. "]The FBI has subpoenaed our books."

25. _____

26. The city's Department of Investigation used hotel rooms specially ["]salted["] with money and jewelry to bait their traps for the criminals.

26. _____

27. "The Lottery[,"] a short story by Shirley Jackson, was discussed in Janet's English class.

27. _____

28. The reporter said[, "]Thank you for the lead on the story," and ran off to track down the source.

28. _____

29. "Was the treaty signed in 1815[?"] the professor asked, "or in 1814?"

29. _____

30. The mayor said, "I guarantee that urban renewal will move forward rapidly[;"] however, I don't believe him.

30. _____

31. Richard Rodriguez writes: "Only when I was able to think of myself as an American, no longer an alien in *gringo* society, could I seek the rights and opportunities necessary for full public individuality[".]

31. _____

32. "Have you seen the rough draft of the article?" asked Jackie[?]

32. _____

33. "You blockhead[,"] screamed Lucy[!]

33. _____

57. PUNCTUATION: Italics and Quotation Marks

(Study 214, Italics, and 215–219, Quotation Marks)

Write the number of the **correct** choice.

Example: A revival of Lerner and Lowe's show (1)*My Fair Lady*
(2)"My Fair Lady" is playing at Proctor's Theater.   ____1____

1. The Broadway hit play (1)*Rent* (2)"Rent" was based on a Puccini opera.   1._____

2. That opera was (1)*La Boheme* (2)"La Boheme."   2._____

3. Keats's poem (1)"Ode on a Grecian Urn" (2) *Ode on a Grecian Urn* is required reading.   3._____

4. Paul Kennedy's book (1)*The Rise and Fall of the Great Powers* (2)"The Rise and Fall of the Great Powers" discusses how nations become politically and militarily dominant.   4._____

5. I just remembered the title of that article in *Prevention* magazine. It is (1)*The New Science of Eating to Get Smart* (2)"The New Science of Eating to Get Smart."   5._____

6. The closing song of the concert was (1)"R-e-s-p-e-c-t" (2)*R-e-s-p-e-c-t.*   6._____

7. (1)*A Haunted House* (2)"A Haunted House" is a short story by Virginia Woolf.   7._____

8. The brevity of Carl Sandburg's poem (1)*Fog* (2)"Fog" appealed to her.   8._____

9. Jack received (1)*A*'s (2) "A's" in three of his classes this fall.   9._____

10. She used too many (1)*and*s (2)"ands" in her introductory speech.   10._____

11. (1)*Science and Religion* (2)"Science and Religion" is an essay by Albert Einstein.   11._____

12. He has purchased tickets for the opera (1)"Faust" (2)*Faust.*   12._____

13. Sharon didn't use a spell-check program and, therefore, unfortunately misspelled (1)*psychology* (2)"psychology" throughout her paper.   13._____

14. Dr. Baylor spent two classes on Wallace Stevens's poem (1)"The Idea of Order at Key West" (2)*The Idea of Order at Key West.*   14._____

15. His favorite newspaper has always been the (1)*Times* (2)"Times."   15._____

16. (1)"Our Town" (2)*Our Town* is a play by Thornton Wilder.   16._____

17. The word *altogether* means (1)"wholly" or "thoroughly." (2)*wholly* or *thoroughly.*   17._____

18. (1)*What Women Want* (2)"What Women Want" is an essay by Margaret Mead.   18._____

19. James Thurber's short story (1)*The Secret Life of Walter Mitty* (2)"The Secret Life of Walter Mitty" amused her.   19._____

20. The Players' Guild will produce Marlowe's (1)*Dr. Faustus* (2)"Dr. Faustus" next month.   20._____

21. Who do you think will ever publish your article (1)*The Joy of Fried Earthworms* (2)"The Joy of Fried Earthworms"?   21._____

22. (1)*Biology: Science of Life* (2)"Biology: Science of Life" is our very expensive textbook for biochemistry class.   22._____

23. One of the first assignments for our African American history classes was James Baldwin's book (1)*Notes of a Native Son* (2)"Notes of a Native Son."   23._____

24. Our film class saw Truffaut's (1)*Shoot the Piano Player* (2)"Shoot the Piano Player" last week.   24. _____

25. She read (1)*Dover Beach,* (2)"Dover Beach," a poem by Matthew Arnold.   25. _____

26. (1)*Pygmalion* (2)"Pygmalion" is a play by George Bernard Shaw.   26. _____

27. You fail to distinguish between the words (1)*range* and *vary.* (2)"range" and "vary."   27. _____

28. I read a poem by Yeats titled (1)"The Cat and the Moon." (2)*The Cat and the Moon.*   28. _____

29. Madeline decided to treat herself by ordering a subscription to (1)*Time* (2)"Time."   29. _____

30. (1)*Fragmented* (2)"Fragmented" is a play by my colleague Prester Pickett.   30. _____

31. I used (1)"Do Lie Detectors Lie?" (2)*Do Lie Detectors Lie?* from *Science* magazine to write my report on famous murder trials.   31. _____

32. Through Kevin Coyne's book (1)"A Day in the Night of America," (2)*A Day in the Night of America,* readers have a chance to see how 7.3 million Americans spend their time working a night shift.   32. _____

33. The last section of the textbook is titled (1)*Paragraphs and Papers.* (2)"Paragraphs and Papers."   33. _____

58. PUNCTUATION: Colon, Dash, Parentheses, and Brackets

(Study 220–221, The Colon; 222, The Dash; 223–224, Parentheses; and 225, Brackets)

Part 1

Write **C** if the colon is used **correctly**.
Write **X** if it is used **incorrectly**.

Example: This bus runs via: Swan Street, Central Avenue, and North Main.　　　　　　　　___X___

1. The President of the International Olympic Committee stepped to the podium and declared: "Let the games begin."　　　1. _____

2. The coach signaled the strategy: we would try a double steal on the next pitch.　　　2. _____

3. Dear Sir:
    My five years' experience as a high school English teacher qualifies me to be the editor of your newsletter.　　　3. _____

4. Dearest Rodney:
    My heart yearns for you so greatly that I can hardly bear the days until we're in each other's arms again.　　　4. _____

5. The following soldiers will fall out for guard duty: Pierce, Romano, Foster, and Sanchez.　　　5. _____

6. The carpenter's tools included: saw, hammer, square, measuring tape, and nails.　　　6. _____

7. College students generally complain about things such as: their professors, the cafeteria food, and their roommates.　　　7. _____

8. She began her letter to Tom with these words: "I'll love you forever!"　　　8. _____

9. Her train reservations were for Tuesday at 3:30 p.m.　　　9. _____

10. The dean demanded that: the coaches, the players, and the training staff meet with him immediately.　　　10. _____

11. Tonight's winning numbers are: 169, 534, and 086.　　　11. _____

12. She was warned that the project would require two qualities: creativity and perseverance.　　　12. _____

13. The project has been delayed: the chairperson has been hospitalized for emergency surgery.　　　13. _____

14. If Smith's book is titled *The World Below the Window: Poems 1937–1997*, must I include both the title and subtitle in my Works Cited list?　　　14. _____

15. I packed my backpack with: bubble bath, a pair of novels, and some comfortable clothes.　　　15. _____

Set off the boldfaced words by inserting the correct punctuation: **dash(es)**, **parentheses**, or **brackets**.

Example: Senator Aikin (**Dem., Maine**) voted for the proposal.

1. In my research paper I quoted Wilson as observing, "His **Fitzgerald's** last years became a remarkable mix of creative growth and physical decline." [Punctuate to show that the boldfaced expression is inserted editorially by the writer of the research paper.]

2. Holmes had deduced **who knew how?** that the man had been born on a moving train during the rainy season. [Punctuate to indicate a sharp interruption.]

3. He will be considered for **this is between you and me, of course** one of the three vice-presidencies in the firm. [Punctuate to indicate merely incidental comment.]

4. I simply told her **and I'm glad I did!** that I would never set foot in her house again. [Punctuate to indicate merely incidental comment.]

5. Campbell's work on *Juvenal* **see reference** is an excellent place to start.

6. At Yosemite National Park we watched the feeding of the bears **from a safe distance, you can be sure.** [Punctuate to achieve a dramatic effect.]

7. Her essay was entitled "The American Medical System and It's **sic** Problems."

8. The rules for using parentheses **see page 7** are not easy to understand.

9. We traveled on foot, in horse-drawn wagons, and occasionally **if we had some spare cash to offer, if the farmers felt sorry for us, or if we could render some service in exchange** atop a motorized tractor. [Punctuate to indicate that this is *not* merely incidental comment.]

10. The statement read: "Enclosed you will find one hundred dollars **$100** to cover damages."

11. David liked one kind of dessert **apple pie.**

12. **Eat, drink, and be merry** gosh, I can hardly wait for senior week.

13. The essay begins: "For more than a hundred years **from 1337 until 1453** the British and French fought a pointless war." [Punctuate to show that the boldfaced expression is inserted editorially.]

14. The concert begins at **by the way, when does the concert begin**?

15. Getting to work at eight o'clock every morning **I don't have to remind you how much I dislike getting up early** seemed almost more than I cared to undertake. [Punctuate to indicate merely incidental comment.]

16. She said, "Two of my friends **one has really serious emotional problems** need psychiatric help." [Punctuate to achieve a dramatic effect.]

17. Within the last year, I have received three **or was it four?** letters from her. [Punctuate to indicate merely incidental comment.]

18. Julius was born in 1900 **?** and came west as a young boy.

59. PUNCTUATION: The Hyphen and the Slash

(Study 226, The Hyphen, and 227, The Slash)

Write **C** if the use or omission of a hyphen or slash is **correct**.
Write **X** if it is **incorrect**.

Example: Seventy six trombones led the big parade.   ___X___

1. Emily Dickinson wrote, "Because I could not stop for **Death, / He** kindly stopped for me."   1. _____

2. "I've **n-n-never** been so **c-c-cold**," stammered Neil, stumbling to shore after the white-water raft overturned.   2. _____

3. He's a true **show-must-go-on** kind of actor.   3. _____

4. One refers to the monarch of Britain as "**His/Her** majesty."   4. _____

5. The speaker was **well known** to everyone connected with administration.   5. _____

6. The **well-known** author was autographing his latest novel in the bookstore today.   6. _____

7. The team averaged over **fifty-thousand** spectators a game.   7. _____

8. The contractor expects to build many **five-** and **six-room** houses this year.   8. _____

9. The senator composed a **carefully-worded** statement for a press conference.   9. _____

10. I sent in my subscription to a new **bi-monthly** magazine.   10. _____

11. Sam's **brother-in-law** delighted in teasing his sister by belching at family dinners.   11. _____

12. We'll have a chance to see two top teams in action at tonight's **Spurs/Pistons** game.   12. _____

13. He made every effort to **recover** the missing gems.   13. _____

14. After the children spilled blueberry syrup on her white sofa, Letitia had to **recover** it.   14. _____

15. At **eighty-four**, Hartley still rides his motorcycle in the mountains on sunny days.   15. _____

16. Charles will run in the **hundred yard** dash next Saturday.   16. _____

17. "The children are not to have any more **c-a-n-d-y**," said Mother.   17. _____

18. After he graduated from college, he became a manager of the **student-owned** bookstore.   18. _____

19. The idea of a **thirty hour** week appealed to the workers.   19. _____

20. Baird played **semi-professional** baseball before going into the major leagues.   20. _____

21. Customers began avoiding the **hot-tempered** clerk in the shoe department.   21. _____

22. Al's main problem is that he lacks **self-confidence**.   22. _____

23. The **brand-new** vacuum cleaner made a loud squealing noise every time we turned it on.   23. _____

24. The word processing software was **brand new**.   24. _____

25. Mr. Pollard's major research interest was **seventeenth-century** French history.   25. _____

60. PUNCTUATION: Review

(Study 201–227, Punctuation)

Write **T** for each statement that is **true**.
Write **F** for each that is **false**.

Example: A period is used at the end of a declarative sentence. _____T_____

1. **Three spaced periods** are used to indicate an omission (ellipsis) in quoted material. 1._____
2. **Possessive personal pronouns** contain an apostrophe. 2._____
3. The **question mark** is always placed inside closing quotation marks. 3._____
4. The sentence "Dellene searched for her friend, Mitch," means that Dellene has only one friend. 4._____
5. A **dash** is used before the author's name on the line below a direct quotation. 5._____
6. **Parentheses** are used to enclose editorial remarks in a direct quotation. 6._____
7. A **restrictive clause** is not set off within commas. 7._____
8. A **semicolon** is used to set off an absolute phrase from the rest of the sentence. 8._____
9. The use of **brackets** around the word *sic* indicates an error occurring in quoted material. 9._____
10. Mild interjections should be followed by an **exclamation point**; strong ones, by a **comma**. 10._____
11. An indirect question is followed by a **period**. 11._____
12. A **semicolon** is used after the expression *Dear Sir*. 12._____
13. The title of a magazine article should be underlined to designate the use of **italics**. 13._____
14. *Ms.* may take a **period** but *Miss* does not. 14._____
15. **Single quotation marks** are used around a quotation that is within another quotation. 15._____
16. Both *Mr. Jones'* and *Mr. Jones's* are acceptable **possessive forms** of *Mr. Jones*. 16._____
17. The title at the head of a composition should be enclosed in **double quotation marks**. 17._____
18. **No apostrophe** is needed in the following greeting: "Merry Christmas from the Palmers." 18._____
19. The **possessive** of *somebody else* is *somebody's else*. 19._____
20. The **possessive** of *mother-in-law* is *mother's-in-law*. 20._____
21. A **semicolon** is normally used between two independent clauses joined by *and* if one or both clauses contain internal commas. 21._____
22. A quotation consisting of several sentences takes **double quotation marks** at the beginning of the first sentence and at the end of the last sentence. 22._____
23. A quotation consisting of several paragraphs takes **double quotation marks** at the beginning and end of each paragraph. 23._____
24. Generally, a **foreign word** is not italicized if it can be found in a reputable American dictionary. 24._____
25. The word *the* is **italicized** in the name of a newspaper or a magazine. 25._____
26. A polite request in the form of a question is followed by a **period**. 26._____

27. **Single quotation marks** may be substituted for double quotation marks around any quoted passage.   27. _____

28. The **comma** is always placed outside quotation marks.   28. _____

29. The **colon** and **semicolon** are always placed outside quotation marks.   29. _____

30. A **comma** is always used to separate the two parts of a compound predicate.   30. _____

31. The expression *such as* is normally followed by a **comma**.   31. _____

32. The **nonsentence** is a legitimate unit of expression and may be followed by a **period**.   32. _____

33. An **exclamation point** and a **question mark** are never used together.   33. _____

34. **Parentheses** are used around words that are to be deleted from a manuscript.   34. _____

35. A **comma** is used between two independent clauses not joined by a coordinating conjunction.   35. _____

36. A **semicolon** is used after the salutation of a friendly letter.   36. _____

37. The subject of a sentence should be separated from the predicate by a **comma**.   37. _____

38. An overuse of **underlining** (italics) for emphasis should be avoided.   38. _____

39. The **contraction** of the words *have not* is written thus: *hav'ent.*   39. _____

40. Nonrestrictive clauses are always set off with **commas**.   40. _____

41. **Double quotation marks** are used around the name of a ship.   41. _____

42. A **comma** is used before the word *then* when it introduces a second independent clause.   42. _____

43. The prefix *semi* always requires a **hyphen**.   43. _____

44. **No comma** is required in the following sentence: "Where do you wish to go?" he asked.   44. _____

45. A **dash** is a legitimate substitute for all other marks of punctuation.   45. _____

46. A **slash** is used to separate two lines of poetry quoted in a running text.   46. _____

47. A **dash** is placed between words used as alternatives.   47. _____

48. Every introductory prepositional phrase is set off by a **comma**.   48. _____

49. An introductory adverbial clause is usually set off with a **comma**.   49. _____

50. A **colon** may be used instead of a **semicolon** between two independent clauses when the second clause is an explanation of the first.   50. _____

61. PUNCTUATION: Review

(Study 201–227, Punctuation)

Part 1

Write **C** if the punctuation in brackets is **correct**.
Write **X** if it is **incorrect**.

Example: The last question on the test [,] counted 30 points.   _____X_____

1. Abner Fenwick found, to his chagrin, that Physics 101 was quite difficult[;] but, because he put in maximum effort, he earned a *B*.   1. _____

2. Pritchett left the casino in despair[,] his last hundred dollars lost on a wrong call in blackjack.   2. _____

3. I wondered why we couldn't get rid of the computer virus[?]   3. _____

4. Dear Dr. Stanley[;] Thank you for your letter of May 10.   4. _____

5. Rafael enjoyed inviting his friends[,] and preparing elaborate meals for them; however, most of his attempts were disasters.   5. _____

6. When the benefits officer described the new medical insurance package, everyone asked, "How much will this new policy cost us["?]   6. _____

7. I remembered the job counselor's remark: "If you send out three hundred inquiry letters in your hometown without even one response, relocate[."]   7. _____

8. "Despite the recession," explained the placement counselor[,] "health care, construction, and teaching still promise an increase in employment opportunities."   8. _____

9. A novella by Conrad, a short story by Lawrence, and some poems of Yeats[,] were all assigned for the last week of the semester.   9. _____

10. Despite the population loss in many Great Plains towns, Fargo, North Dakota[,] is thriving.   10. _____

11. Why is it that other children seem to behave better than our[']s?   11. _____

12. The relief workers specifically requested food, blankets, and children['s] clothing.   12. _____

13. Approximately seven million Americans visit their doctor each year[;] seeking an answer for why they feel so tired.   13. _____

14. Whenever he speaks, he's inclined to use too many *and-uh*[']s between sentences.   14. _____

15. The auditor requested to review[:] the medical receipts, our child-care expenses, and any deductions for home improvement.   15. _____

16. The last employee to leave the office is responsible for the following[,] turning off the machines, extinguishing all lights, and locking all executives' office doors.   16. _____

17. Everywhere there were crowds shouting anti[-]American slogans.   17. _____

18. Private colleges and universities are concerned about dwindling enrollment[;] because their tuition costs continue to climb while requests for substantial financial aid are also increasing.   18. _____

19. During the whole wretched ordeal of his doctoral exams[;] Charles remained outwardly calm.   19. _____

20. More than twenty minutes were cut from the original version of the film[,] the producers told neither the director nor the writer.   20. _____

21. The mock-epic poem "Casey at the Bat" was first published June 3, 1888[,] in the *Examiner*.   21. _____

22. We were married on June 5, 2003[,] in Lubbock, Texas.   22. _____

23. The temperature sinking fast as dusk approached[;] we decided to seek shelter for the night.   23. _____

24. By the year 2000, only about half of Americans entering the workforce were native born and of European stock[;] thus this country is truly becoming a multiracial society.   24. _____

25. My only cousin[,] who is in the U.S. Air Force[,] is stationed in the Arctic.   25. _____

26. Any U.S. Air Force officer[,] who is stationed in the Arctic[,] receives extra pay.   26. _____

27. Hey! Did you find a biology book in this classroom[?!]   27. _____

28. Charles Goodyear, the man who gave the world vulcanized rubber, personified the qualities of the classic American inventor[:] he spent nine years experimenting to find a waterproof rubber that would be resistant to extreme temperatures.   28. _____

29. To reach the Museum of Natural History you take the D train to Columbus Circle[;] then you transfer to the C train.   29. _____

30. The first well-known grocery store group was[,] the Atlantic and Pacific Tea Company, founded in 1859.   30. _____

31. Fernando jumped and squealed with delight[,] because he found a new pair of roller blades under his bed as a present from his family's Three Kings celebration.   31. _____

32. The movies[,] that I prefer to see[,] always have happy endings.   32. _____

33. At the powwow Anna and her friends entered the Fancy Shawl Dance competition[;] for they wanted to dance in their new dresses and moccasins.   33. _____

Part 2

In the following paragraphs, **insert** the correct punctuation mark(s) in each set of brackets. If no punctuation is needed, leave the brackets empty.

Example: Shawaun said[, "]Do it yourself[,"] and stormed out.

1. The published writings of F. Scott Fitzgerald[ ] range from youthful short stories[ ] such as [ ]Bernice Bobs Her Hair[ ] to novels of well[ ]to[ ]do Long Islanders[ ] American expatriates[ ] and Hollywood movie moguls. His most famous novel[ ] [The Great Gatsby][ ] set on Long Island[ ] depicts the rise and fall[ ] of a [nouveau-riche] young man[ ] who was born James Gatz[ ] in the Midwest. Gatsby[ ]s failed attempt to recapture his past has captivated Americans[ ]it also became a play and a film[ ]for nearly four generations.

2. Sojourner Truth [ ]c. 1797–1883[ ] was born a slave[ ] and was never taught to read or write[ ] but she became a noted abolitionist and campaigner for women[ ]s rights. How could such a transformation occur[ ] This remarkable woman[ ] who was born in upstate New York[ ] was originally named Isabella. After she was freed[ ] she worked as a servant in New York City[ ] during which time she heard voices from heaven. Responding to the voices[ ] she changed her name to Sojourner Truth [ ][sojourner] means [ ]one who stops briefly at a place[ ][ ] and began traveling through the North. She soon gained fame as a fiery[ ] articulate[ ] and moving public speaker. In 1878 a book was written about her[ ] [Narrative of Sojourner Truth][ ] by Olive Gilbert. What an inspiration Sojourner Truth has been to all[ ] who believe in equality[ ]

62. MECHANICS: Capitals

(Study 301–303, Capitalization)

Write **C** if the boldfaced word(s) are **correct** in use or omission of capital letters.
Write **X** if the word(s) are **incorrect**.

Example: Cajuns speak a dialect of **french**. ___X___

1. Hundreds attended the **Muslim** prayer service. 1. ____

2. The recession changed many seniors' plans to attend an expensive **College**. 2. ____

3. The **turkish** bath is closed. 3. ____

4. She wanted to become a Methodist **Minister**. 4. ____

5. When will **Congress** convene? 5. ____

6. She is a **Junior** at the University of Houston. 6. ____

7. Gregory looked forward eagerly to visiting his **Mother-in-Law.** 7. ____

8. He always disliked **Calculus**. 8. ____

9. Joe constantly reads about the **Civil War.** 9. ____

10. I made an appointment with **Professor** Allen. 10. ____

11. She met three **Professors** today. 11. ____

12. "Did you save your paper on the disk?" **she** asked. 12. ____

13. Each **Spring** I try a new sport. 13. ____

14. The deaths were reported in the *Times*. 14. ____

15. I worked in the **Southwest**. 15. ____

16. Her **Aunt Miriam** has returned. 16. ____

17. He's late for his **anthropology** class. 17. ____

18. John was **Secretary** of his class. 18. ____

19. Woods was promoted to **Major**. 19. ____

20. The bookstore has a special sale on Hewlett-Packard **Computers**. 20. ____

21. I enrolled in **english** and physics. 21. ____

22. He began his letter with "My **Dear** Mrs. Johnson." 22. ____

23. He ended it with "Yours **Truly**." 23. ____

24. We once lived in the **Northwest**. 24. ____

25. I passed German but failed **Biology**. 25. ____

26. He plans to attend **Medical School** next year. 26. ____

27. Harold believes there is life on **venus**. 27. ____

28. I asked **Mother** for some legal advice. 28. ____

29. He goes to **Roosevelt High School**. 29. ____

30. Has the **senate** in Washington elected a majority leader yet? 30. ____

31. The year that actually began the **twenty-first century** was 2001, not 2000. 31. ____

32. I listen to **wfbg** every morning. 32. ____

33. We are planning a picnic on Memorial **day**. 33. ____

34. I spent the fall break with my **Aunt**. 34. ____

35. Her favorite subject is **German**. 35. ____

36. The tourists visited **Niagara Falls**. 36. ____

37. The **President's** veto of the most recent bill has angered Congress. 37. ____

38. He enrolled in **Physics 215**. 38. ____

39. This is a Lutheran **Church**. 39. ____

40. I am writing a book; **My** editor wants the first chapter soon. 40. ____

41. This is **NOT** my idea of fun. 41. ____

42. I think **mother nature** was particularly cruel this winter. 42. ____

43. She earned a **Ph.D.** degree. 43. ____

44. The **Championship Fight** was a disappointment. 44. ____

45. It is a **Jewish** custom for men to wear skull caps during worship. 45. ____

46. His grandfather fought in the Korean **war**. 46. ____

47. The chairperson of the **Department of History** is Dr. Mo.   47. ____

48. He said simply, "**my** name is Bond."   48. ____

49. "**Sexual Harassment: The Price of Silence**" is a chapter from my composition reader.   49. ____

50. She spent her **Thanksgiving** vacation in Iowa with her family.   50. ____

63. MECHANICS: Capitals

(Study 301–303, Capitalization)

In the first blank write the number of the **first** correct choice (**1** or **2**).
In the second blank write the number of the **second** correct choice (**3** or **4**).

Example: Wandering (1)**West** (2)**west**, Max met (3)**Milly** (4)**milly**.   <u>2</u> <u>3</u>

1. Investors lost millions in accounting scandals at the Megabux (1)**Company** (2)**company**, which produces Zoomfast (3)**Cars** (4)**cars**.   1. ____ ____

2. Her (1)**Father** (2)**father** went (3)**South** (4)**south** on business.   2. ____ ____

3. The new (1)**College** (2)**college** is seeking a (3)**Dean** (4)**dean**.   3. ____ ____

4. Children are taught to begin letters with "My (1)**Dear** (2)**dear** (3)**Sir** (4)**sir**."   4. ____ ____

5. Business letters often end with "Very (1)**Truly** (2)**truly** (3)**Yours** (4)**yours**."   5. ____ ____

6. After (1)**Church** (2)**church**, we walked across the Brooklyn (3)**Bridge** (4)**bridge**.   6. ____ ____

7. The (1)**Politician** (2)**politician** declared that the protester was (3)**Un-American** (4)**un-American**.   7. ____ ____

8. The young (1)**Lieutenant** (2)**lieutenant** prayed to the (3)**Lord** (4)**lord** for courage in the battle.   8. ____ ____

9. My (1)**Cousin** (2)**cousin** now lives in the (3)**East** (4)**east**.   9. ____ ____

10. The (1)**President** (2)**president** addresses (3)**Congress** (4)**congress** tomorrow.   10. ____ ____

11. Joan Bailey, (1)**M.D.**, (2)**m.d.**, once taught (3)**Biology** (4)**biology**.   11. ____ ____

12. Dr. Mikasa, (1)**Professor** (2)**professor** of (3)**English** (4)**english**, is writing a murder mystery.   12. ____ ____

13. The (1)**Comet** (2)**comet** can be seen just below (3)**The Big Dipper** (4)**the Big Dipper**.   13. ____ ____

14. "I'm also a graduate of North Harris (1)**College** (2)**college**," (3)**She** (4)**she** added.   14. ____ ____

15. The (1)**Rabbi** (2)**rabbi** of (3)**Temple** (4)**temple** Beth Emeth is a leader in interfaith cooperation.   15. ____ ____

16. Vera disagreed with the review of "(1)**The** (2)**the** War Chronicles" in (3)*The* (4)*the* New York Times.   16. ____ ____

17. The club (1)**Treasurer** (2)**treasurer** said that the financial report was "(3)**Almost** (4)**almost** complete."   17. ____ ____

18. The (1)**Girl Scout** (2)**girl scout** leader pointed out the (3)**Milky Way** (4)**milky way** to her troop.   18. ____ ____

19. Students use the textbook *Writing (1)For (2)for Audience (3)And (4)and Purpose.*   19. ____ ____

20. Educational Support Services is in (1)**Room** (2)**room** 110 of Yost (3)**Hall** (4)**hall**.   20. ____ ____

21. At the (1)**Battle** (2)**battle** of Gettysburg, Confederate troops actually approached from (3)**North** (4)**north** of the town.   21. ____ ____

22. I think it's never (1)**O.K.** (2)**o.k.** to ignore a summons from the (3)**Police** (4)**police**.   22. ____ ____

23. The correspondent described the (1)**Pope** (2)**pope** as looking "(3)**Frail** (4)**frail** and unsteady."   23. ____ ____

24. "Maria, look up at the (1)**Moon** (2)**moon**," Guido said softly, "(3)**And** (4)**and** drink in its beauty."   24. ____ ____

25. "Maria, look up at (1)**Venus** (2)**venus**," Guido said softly. "(3)**Drink** (4)**drink** in its beauty."   25. ____ ____

64. MECHANICS: Numbers and Abbreviations

(Study 305–307, Numbers, and 308–309, Abbreviations)

Write the number of the **correct** choice.

Example: The book was (1)**3** (2)**three** days overdue.   _____2_____

1. (1)**135** (2)**One hundred thirty-five** votes was the official margin of victory.   1. _____

2. The odometer showed that it was (1)**5½** (2)**five and one-half** miles from the campus to the beach.   2. _____

3. (1)**Prof.** (2)**Professor** Hilton teaches Asian philosophy.   3. _____

4. Their parents went to (1)**Fla.** (2)**Florida** for the winter.   4. _____

5. Builders are still reluctant to have a (1)**thirteenth** (2)**13th** floor in any new buildings.   5. _____

6. The exam will be held at noon on (1)**Fri.** (2)**Friday**.   6. _____

7. The (1)**P.O.** (2)**post office** on campus always has a long line of international students mailing letters and packages to their friends and families.   7. _____

8. Judd has an interview with the Sherwin Williams (1)**Co.** (2)**Company**.   8. _____

9. Nicole will study in Germany, (1)**Eng.** (2)**England**, and Sweden next year.   9. _____

10. Evan Booster, (1)**M.D.**, (2)**medical doctor,** is my physician.   10. _____

11. Frank jumped 22 feet, (1)**3** (2)**three** inches at the Saturday meet.   11. _____

12. For the laboratory, the department purchased permanent markers, legal pads, pencils, (1)**etc.** (2)**and other office supplies**.   12. _____

13. For (1)**Xmas** (2)**Christmas**, the Fords planned a quiet family gathering rather than their usual ski holiday.   13. _____

14. Travis needed to leave for work at exactly 8:00 (1)**a.m.** (2)**o'clock**.   14. _____

15. John's stipend was (1)**$2,145** (2)**two thousand one hundred forty-five dollars**.   15. _____

16. She will graduate from medical school June (1)**2**, (2)**2nd**, 2006.   16. _____

17. He and his family moved to Vermont last (1)**Feb.** (2)**February**, didn't they?   17. _____

18. Over (1)**900** (2)**nine hundred** students attend Roosevelt Junior High School.   18. _____

19. Brad loved all of his (1)**phys. ed.** (2)**physical education** electives.   19. _____

20. Next year, the convention will be held on April (1)**19**, (2)**19th**, (3)**nineteenth**, in Burlington.   20. _____

21. The service included an inspiring homily by the (1)**Rev.** (2)**Reverend** Spooner.   21. _____

22. The lottery prize has reached an astonishing (1)**twenty-four million dollars** (2)**$24 million**.   22. _____

23. The family next door adopted a (1)**two-month-old** (2)**2-month-old** baby girl from China.   23. _____

24. We had an opportunity to meet (1)**Sen.** (2)**Senator** Lester at the convention.   24. _____

25. The diagram was on (1)**pg.** (2)**page** 44.   25. _____

26. One of my friends will do her student teaching in (1)**TX.** (2)**Texas** this spring.   26. _____

27. When we offered tickets to a baseball game for our raffle, we had (1)**one-third** (2)**1/3rd** of the employees purchase tickets. 27. _____

28. Jack's dissertation was (1)**two hundred fifty** (2)**250** pages. 28. _____

29. The plane expected from (1)**LA early this a.m.** (2)**Los Angeles early this morning** is late. 29. _____

30. The bus arrives at 10:55 a.m. and leaves at (1)**11:00** (2)**eleven** a.m. 30. _____

31. The Elks Club raised $265, The Moose $126, and the Beavers Lodge (1)**ninety dollars** (2)**$90**. 31. _____

32. Rachel's name was (1)**twenty-sixth** (2)**26th** on the list of high school graduates. 32. _____

33. Private Bailey wanted a (1)**3-day** (2)**three-day** pass to see Lorena. 33. _____

65. MECHANICS: Capitals, Numbers, and Abbreviations

(Study 301–303, Capitalization; 305–307, Numbers; and 308–309, Abbreviations)

In the first blank write the number of the **first** correct choice (**1** or **2**).
In the second blank write the number of the **second** correct choice (**3** or **4**).

Example: I have only (1)**three and one-half** (2)**3½** years until (3)**Graduation** (4)**graduation**.   <u>2</u>   <u>4</u>

1. After much squabbling (1)**Congress** (2)**congress** finally passed the Tax Reduction (3)**Act** (4)**act**.   1. ____ ____

2. Many of those who died when (1)*The Titanic* (2)the *Titanic* went down are buried in a (3)**Cemetery** (4)**cemetery** in Halifax, Nova Scotia.   2. ____ ____

3. My (1)**Supervisor** (2)**supervisor** said our presentation was (3)**"Insightful!"** (4)**"insightful."**   3. ____ ____

4. "I expect," he said, (1)**"To** (2)**"to** get an *A* in my (3)**Chem.** (4)**chemistry** class."   4. ____ ____

5. On June (1)**6,** (2)**6th,** 2006, she spoke at St. Paul's (3)**High School** (4)**high school.**   5. ____ ____

6. The new college (1)**President** (2)**president** greeted the (3)**Alumni** (4)**alumni** during the graduation ceremonies.   6. ____ ____

7. An (1)**American Flag** (2)**American flag** from the World Trade (3)**Center** (4)**center** was flown at the memorial service.   7. ____ ____

8. The (1)**treasurer** (2)**Treasurer** of the (3)**Junior Accountants' Club** (4)**junior accountants' club** has absconded with our dues.   8. ____ ____

9. (1)**308** (2)**Three hundred eight** students passed the test out of (3)**427** (4)**four hundred twenty-seven** who took it.   9. ____ ____

10. She likes her (1)**english** (2)**English** and (3)**science** (4)**Science** classes.   10. ____ ____

11. I soon realized that (1)**spring** (2)**Spring** means rain, rain, and more rain in northeastern (3)**Ohio** (4)**ohio.**   11. ____ ____

12. Industry in the (1)**South** (2)**south** is described in this month's (3)*Fortune* (4)*fortune* magazine.   12. ____ ____

13. Victor is going to take an (1)**english** (2)**English** course this semester instead of one in (3)**History** (4)**history.**   13. ____ ____

14. She was ecstatic; (1)**Her** (2)**her** boyfriend had just bought her a 2004 General Motors (3)**Pickup Truck** (4)**pickup truck.**   14. ____ ____

15. The new (1)**doctor** (2)**Doctor** has opened an office on Main (3)**Street** (4)**street.**   15. ____ ____

16. The (1)**korean** (2)**Korean** students have planned their (3)**3rd** (4)**third** annual International Dinner.   16. ____ ____

17. I spent (1)**New Year's Day** (2)**new year's day** with (3)**mother** (4)**Mother.**   17. ____ ____

18. Her (1)**Japanese** (2)**japanese** instructor is touring the American (3)**Midwest** (4)**midwest** over the summer.   18. ____ ____

19. I need a (1)**Psychology** (2)**psychology** book from the (3)**Library** (4)**library.**   19. ____ ____

20. The (1)**class** (2)**Class** of '08 honored the (3)**Dean of Men** (4)**dean of men.**   20. ____ ____

21. Leslie enrolled in (1)**Doctor** (2)**Dr.** Newell's history course; she is majoring in (3)**social science** (4)**Social Science.**   21. ____ ____

22. Jim moved to eastern Arizona; (1)**He** (2)**he** bought over (3)**400** (4)**four hundred** acres of land. 22. ____ ____

23. She knows (1)**four** (2)**4** students who are going to (3)**College** (4)**college** this fall. 23. ____ ____

24. Many (1)**hispanic** (2)**Hispanic** students have immigrated to this (3)**country** (4)**Country** because of political turmoil in their homelands. 24. ____ ____

25. In (1)**Chapter four** (2)**chapter 4**, (3)**Chief Inspector Morse** (4)**chief inspector Morse** discovers the professor's body. 25. ____ ____

66. SPELLING

(Study 310–314, Spelling)

Write the number of the **correctly spelled** word.

Example: A knowledge of (1)**grammar** (2)**grammer** is helpful.   ___1___

1. A large (1)**quantity** (2)**quanity** of illegal drugs was seized by customs inspectors at the border.   1. _____

2. The company's lawyers said that it was (1)**alright** (2)**all right** to sign the contract.   2. _____

3. No one thought that a romance would (1)**develope** (2)**develop** between those two.   3. _____

4. Mrs. Smith will not (1)**acknowlege** (2)**acknowledge** whether she received the check.   4. _____

5. I love to (1)**surprise** (2)**suprise** the children with small presents.   5. _____

6. After three well-played quarters, the Bruins had a (1)**disasterous** (2)**disastrous** fourth quarter.   6. _____

7. One of the volunteers will be (1)**ninety** (2)**ninty** (3)**nintey** years old next week.   7. _____

8. The salary will depend on how (1)**competant** (2)**competent** the employee is.   8. _____

9. I loved listening to Grandpa's tales about his childhood because he always (1)**exagerated** (2)**exaggerated** the details.   9. _____

10. It's important to accept valid (1)**criticism** (2)**critcism** without taking the comments personally.   10. _____

11. It was (1)**ridiculous** (2)**rediculous** to expect Fudgley to arrive on time.   11. _____

12. (1)**Approximately** (2)**Approximatly** fifty families attended the adoption support group meeting.   12. _____

13. The murder was a (1)**tradegy** (2)**tragedy** (3)**tradgedy** felt by the entire community.   13. _____

14. The Statue of Liberty is a (1)**symbel** (2)**symbol** of the United States.   14. _____

15. Everyone could hear the (1)**argument** (2)**arguement** between the two young lovers.   15. _____

16. Tim asked several questions because he wasn't sure what the professor (1)**ment** (2)**meant** by a "term paper of reasonable length."   16. _____

17. The professor was offended by the (1)**ommission** (2)**omission** of his research data.   17. _____

18. Carrying a portable telephone seems a (1)**necessary** (2)**neccessary** precaution.   18. _____

19. Every time I visit Aunt Nan, she likes to (1)**reminisce** (2)**reminice** about her youth.   19. _____

20. Meeting with a tutor for an hour before the examination was a (1)**desperate** (2)**desparate** attempt by Tom to pass his math class.   20. _____

21. Susan was excited about her (1)**nineth**- (2)**ninth**-grade graduation ceremony.   21. _____

22. Sally needed a lot of (1)**repetition** (2)**repitition** in order to memorize the formulas for her next chemistry test.   22. _____

23. How (1)**definite** (2)**defenite** is their decision to return to Texas?   23. _____

24. The weight loss program offered a (1)**guarantee** (2)**garantee** that I would lose at least ten pounds.   24. _____

25. Jake hoped his temporary job would become a (1)**permenent** (2)**permanent** position.   25. _____

26. I always bring back a (1)**souvenir** (2)**suvinir** for my children when I travel on business.   26. _____

27. We were glad that the (1)**auxilary** (2)**auxiliary** lights came on during the severe thunderstorm.   27. _____

28. Rodney, unfortunately, had not (1)**fulfilled** (2)**fullfilled** the requirements for graduation.   28. _____

29. In our state, students in the (1)**twelth** (2)**twelfth** grade must pass a basic skills test.   29. _____

30. This year, our five-year-old son began to question the (1)**existance** (2)**existence** of the tooth fairy.   30. _____

31. When Loretta turned (1)**forty** (2)**fourty**, her office mates filled her office with balloons and threw her a surprise party.   31. _____

32. Alex said that one of the worst aspects of life in Russia was the government's (1)**suppression** (2)**suppresion** of religious activity.   32. _____

33. Jack (1)**use to** (2)**used to** run a mile five times a week.   33. _____

34. Unfortunately, I find chocolate—any chocolate—(1)**irresistable** (2)**irresistible**.   34. _____

35. All three of my children are heading towards (1)**adolescence** (2)**adolesence**.   35. _____

36. The (1)**phychologist** (2)**psychologist** arranged a group program for procrastinators.   36. _____

37. My mother's suggestion actually seemed quite (1)**sensible** (2)**sensable**.   37. _____

38. The (1)**Sophomore** (2)**Sophmore** Class voted to sponsor a dance next month.   38. _____

39. They chose the restaurant that had a (1)**late-nite** (2)**late-night** special.   39. _____

40. The high school's star athlete was a (1)**conscientous** (2)**conscientious** student.   40. _____

41. The (1)**rythm** (2)**rhythm** of the song was perfect for our skating routine.   41. _____

42. My friend decided to (1)**persue** (2)**pursue** a degree in sociology.   42. _____

43. I don't have time for (1)**questionaires** (2)**questionnaires**.   43. _____

44. Robert's (1)**perseverance** (2)**perserverence** led to his ultimate success in the theater.   44. _____

45. She has a (1)**tendancy** (2)**tendency** to do her best work early in the day.   45. _____

46. Her services had become (1)**indispensible** (2)**indispensable** to the firm.   46. _____

47. A reception was held for students having an (1)**excellent** (2)**excellant** scholastic record.   47. _____

48. Glen hopes to add (1)**playright** (2)**playwright** (3)**playwrite** to his list of professional credits.   48. _____

49. You will find no (1)**prejudice** (2)**predjudice** in our organization.   49. _____

50. Caldwell is (1)**suppose to** (2)**supposed to** deliver the lumber sometime today.   50. _____

67. SPELLING

(Study 310–314, Spelling)

If the word is spelled **incorrectly**, write the **correct spelling** in the blank.
If the word is spelled **correctly**, leave the blank empty.

Examples: hindrance _____

vaccum   ___vacuum___

1. unusualy	1._____	26. sincereley	26._____
2. oppinion	2._____	27. saftey	27._____
3. criticize	3._____	28. synonim	28._____
4. familar	4._____	29. catagory	29._____
5. proceedure	5._____	30. imaginery	30._____
6. thru	6._____	31. managment	31._____
7. pursue	7._____	32. amateur	32._____
8. accross	8._____	33. reguler	33._____
9. confident	9._____	34. hygiene	34._____
10. maneuver	10._____	35. cemetery	35._____
11. relieve	11._____	36. heros	36._____
12. absense	12._____	37. bookkeeper	37._____
13. sacrefice	13._____	38. monkeys	38._____
14. mischievious	14._____	39. persistant	39._____
15. prevalent	15._____	40. curiosity	40._____
16. parallel	16._____	41. stimulent	41._____
17. noticeable	17._____	42. villian	42._____
18. disasterous	18._____	43. knowledge	43._____
19. indepindent	19._____	44. optimism	44._____
20. bussiness	20._____	45. embarass	45._____
21. acquire	21._____	46. eighth	46._____
22. truly	22._____	47. maintenence	47._____
23. government	23._____	48. father-in-laws	48._____
24. appologize	24._____	49. happyness	49._____
25. controlling	25._____	50. crisises	50._____

68. SPELLING

(Study 310–314, Spelling)

Part 1

In the blank, write the **missing letter(s)** (if any) in the word.
If no letter is missing, leave the blank empty.

Examples: gramm_*a*_r
ath_____lete

1. suppr_____ssion
2. piano_____s
3. kni_____s [sharp instruments]
4. bus_____ly
5. defin_____te
6. permiss_____ble
7. perm_____nent
8. guid_____nce
9. d_____scription
10. fascinat_____ing
11. gu_____rantee
12. abs_____nce
13. appar_____nt
14. hindr_____nce
15. crit_____cism
16. benefit_____ed
17. confer_____ed
18. am_____teur
19. argu_____ment
20. me_____nt

21. math_____matics
22. pre_____judice
23. par_____llel
24. erron_____ous
25. prev_____lent
26. rest_____urant
27. rep_____tition
28. nec_____ssary
29. sacr_____fice
30. compet_____nt
31. com_____ing [arriving]
32. tru_____ly
33. chimn_____s
34. excell_____nt
35. sch_____dule
36. independ_____nt
37. immediat_____ly
38. consc_____entious
39. op_____ortunity
40. dis_____atisfied

In the blank, write the **missing letters** in each word: **ie** or **ei**.

Example: bel _ie_ ve

1. h____r
2. ach____ve
3. rec____ve
4. c____ling
5. w____rd

6. v____n
7. ch____f
8. l____sure
9. hyg____ne
10. w____gh

69. MECHANICS, WITH SPELLING: Review

(Study 301–314, Mechanics, with Spelling)

In each of the following paragraphs, correct all errors in **capitalization**, **number form**, **abbreviations**, **syllabication**, and **spelling**. Cross out the incorrect form and write the correct form above it.

(Collaborative option: Students work in pairs or small groups to find and correct errors.)

1. Martha's Vineyard is an Island off cape Cod, Mass., that covers aproximately two hundred sixty sq. kilometers. The first europeans to settle there were the English, in 1642. In the 18th Century Fishing and Whaling came into existance as its cheif sources of employment. By the 18 ninteys its developement as a Summer resort was under way. Wealthy people from N.Y. and Boston vacationed on its beaches and sailed around its harbors. John D. Rock-efeller, jr., and other socialites visited there, usually in Aug., the most populer vacation month. It was a favorite spot of the Kennedy Family. Today the year-round population is about 6 thousand. Its communitys include Oak Bluffs, Tisbury, and W. Tisbury. Martha's Vineyard also contains a State Forest.

2. A hurricane is a cyclone that arises in the Tropics, with winds exceeding seventy-five mph, or 121 kilometers per hour. The term *Hurricane* is usually applied to cyclones in the N. Atlantic ocean, whereas those in the western Pacific are called typhoons. Some hurricanes, however, arise in the eastern Pacific, off the West coast of Mexico, and move Northeast. In an average yr. three point five hurricanes will form off the east coast of North America, maturing in the Caribbean sea or the gulf of Mexico. Such hurricanes are most prevelent in Sept. One of the most destructive of these storms slammed into the United States in 1938, causing 100s of deaths in the Northeast. In the nineteen-nineties Hurricane Andrew devastated southern Fla., including Everglades national park. Homes, Churches, schools, and wharfs were ripped apart. Hurricanes can last from 1 to thirty days, weakening as they pass over land. Over the warm Ocean, however, their fury intensifies, and they often generate enormous waves that engulf Coastal areas. To learn more about hurricanes, read *Hurricanes, Their Nature And History.*

3. Turkey is a unique Country. Though partly in Europe, it is ninety seven % in Asia; thus it combines elements of European, middle eastern, and Asiatic cultures. Though the country's Capital is Ankara, its most-famous city is Istanbul, which was for 100s of yrs. called Constantinople and before that Byzantium. To the west of Turkey lies the Aegean sea; to the s.e. lie Iran, Iraq, & Syria. The vast majority of Turks are Muslim, but there are also small

numbers of christians and Spanish Speaking Jews. Modern Turkey came into being after the downfall of the

Ottoman empire in world war I; its present boundaries were established by the treaty of Lausanne in nineteen

twenty-three. 17 years later the nation switched from the arabic to the roman Alphabet. In Government Turkey has

a two house Legislature and a head of State.

70. WORD CHOICE: Conciseness, Clarity, and Originality

(Study 401, Conciseness, Clarity, and Originality)

Rewrite each sentence in the space below it, **replacing** or **eliminating** all redundant, overblown, vague, or clichéd expressions. You may use a dictionary, and you may invent specifics if necessary.

Examples: We find our general consensus of opinion to be that the governor should resign.
Our consensus is that the governor should resign.

She looked really nice.
She wore jet-black jeans and a trim white blouse, and her broad smile would melt an iceberg.

(Collaborative option: Students work in pairs or small groups to examine sentences and suggest improvements.)

1. The director she believes that within a few months that she can increase profits by 25 percent.

   _____

   _____

2. As a small child of three years of age, I was allowed outside to play only during the hours from eight to eleven a.m. in the morning and from three to five p.m. in the afternoon.

   _____

   _____

3. Lady Macbeth returned back to the deadly murder scene to leave the daggers beside the grooms.

   _____

   _____

4. In the Bible it says that we should not make a judgment about others.

   _____

   _____

5. Except for the fact that my grandmother is on Medicaid, she would not be able to afford living in her very unique senior citizens' residential facility.

   _____

   _____

6. The deplorable condition of business is due to the nature of the current conditions relevant to the economic situation.

   _____

   _____

7. The thing in question at this point in time is whether the initial phase of the operation is proceeding with a sufficient degree of efficiency.

_____

_____

8. She jumped off of the wall and continued on down the lane so that she could meet up with me outside of my domicile.

_____

_____

9. The house was blue in color and octagonal in shape.

_____

_____

10. She couldn't hardly lose her way, due to the fact that the road was intensely illuminated.

_____

_____

11. On the basis of this report, it leads me to come to the conclusion that the recruitment process at this office is in need of amelioration.

_____

_____

12. The next thing our speaker will speak about is the problem of the transportation situation.

_____

_____

13. We are voting to elect Barnett because of the fact that she has a great attitude and so many nice qualities.

_____

_____

14. In this day and age things can happen out of a clear blue sky, quick as a wink, to upset one's apple cart.

_____

_____

15. The patient fell on his gluteus maximus when we IV'd him in pre-op.

_____

_____

16. We have reached the conclusion that the men and women who fly our planes need further training in finding their way from one location to another.

_____

_____

17. I saw my father stumble out of the drinking establishment and walk in an unsteady way down the alley.

_____

_____

18. It is a known fact that people who have undergone the training process in emergency rescue procedures necessarily have to know how to take over in a crisis situation.

_____

_____

19. In the event that inclement weather becomes a factor, the game may be postponed until a later date.

_____

_____

20. We have lost our way, but however, we may connect up with our friends if we utilize our heads to find the right road.

_____

_____

71. WORD CHOICE: Standard, Appropriate English

(Study 402, Standard, Appropriate English)

Part 1

Write the number of the **correct** choice (use standard, formal American English).

Example: Lincoln had no doubt (1)**but that** (2)**that** the South would secede.   _____2_____

1. The dictator determined to attack across the border (1)**irregardless** (2)**regardless** of the consequences.   1. _____

2. That year Einstein conceived his most (1)**revolutionary** (2)**terrific** theory, that of general relativity.   2. _____

3. (1)**Hopefully,** (2)**We hope that** the instructor will post our grades before we leave for the holidays.   3. _____

4. Juan used (1)**these kind of tools** (2)**these kinds of tools** to repair the roof.   4. _____

5. We were disappointed (1)**somewhat** (2)**some** at the poor quality of the color printer.   5. _____

6. We heard the same report (1)**everywhere** (2)**everywheres** we traveled.   6. _____

7. Eileen and Bob (1)**got married** (2)**were married** on a tropical beach at sunrise.   7. _____

8. Do (1)**try to** (2)**try and** spend the night with us when you are in town.   8. _____

9. The diplomat was (1)**most** (2)**almost** at the end of her patience.   9. _____

10. I (1)**had ought** (2)**ought** to have let her know the time of my arrival.   10. _____

11. Will you be sure to (1)**contact** (2)**telephone** me tomorrow?   11. _____

12. He (1)**seldom ever** (2)**hardly ever** writes to his sister.   12. _____

13. The (1)**children** (2)**kids** in my class are interested in the field trip.   13. _____

14. The lawyer wasn't (1)**enthused** (2)**enthusiastic** about her new case.   14. _____

15. The supervisor (1)**should of** (2)**should have** rewritten the memo.   15. _____

16. The van needed a new battery (1)**besides** (2) **plus** an oil change.   16. _____

Write **C** if the boldfaced expression is **correct**.
Write **X** if it is **incorrect**.

Example: Lincoln had no doubt **but that** the
South would secede.   __X__

1. You **hadn't ought** to sneak into the show.   1. ____

2. We were **plenty** surprised by the outcome of our survey.   2. ____

3. He studied **a lot** for the biology lab exam.   3. ____

4. Susan is **awfully** depressed.   4. ____

5. I **sure** am sore from my exercise class.   5. ____

6. He **better** get here before noon.   6. ____

7. She is a **real** hard worker.   7. ____

8. I admire **that kind** of initiative.   8. ____

9. He has **plenty** of opportunities for earning money.   9. ____

10. The damage was **nowhere near** as severe as it was originally estimated to be.   10. ____

11. His finances are in bad **shape.**   11. ____

12. **Due to** the pollution levels, the city banned incinerators.   12. ____

13. The horrors of war drove him **mad.**   13. ____

14. She was **terribly** pleased at winning the contest.   14. ____

15. Be sure **and** review your class notes before the examination.   15. ____

16. I am a neat person, **aren't I**?   16. ____

17. He wrote essays, short stories, **etc.**   17. ____

18. There was a **bunch** of people in the waiting room.   18. ____

19. Sue's balloon had **bursted**.   19. ____

20. I am sure that he will be **O.K.**   20. ____

21. The students created a mock exam **theirselves**.   21. ____

22. They plan to visit Munich **and/or** Salzburg.   22. ____

23. **Being as how** the bank was closed, Sonya could not withdraw her money.   23. ____

24. She needed the money so **badly** that she cried.   24. ____

25. This has been an auspicious day for you and **me**.   25. ____

26. He **couldn't help but** wonder at her attitude.   26. ____

27. When the **cops** came, everyone was relieved.   27. ____

28. Her **funny** way of speaking made them wonder where she had grown up.   28. ____

29. January employment figures had an **impact** on the stock market.   29. ____

30. His proposal made her **so** happy.   30. ____

31. Do you plan to go to **that there** party?   31. ____

32. We tried to find Illyria, but there was **no such place**.   32. ____

33. The vote was 97–31, **so** the treaty was approved.   33. ____

34. They **have got** a solution to the puzzle.   34. ____

72. WORD CHOICE: Standard, Appropriate English

(Study 402, Standard, Appropriate English)

Most of the following sentences contain one or more lapses from standard, formal English. In the blanks below, **rewrite** the sentence in standard, formal English. If a sentence needs no change, leave the blanks empty.

Example: You better not bring drugs to campus, seeing as how this is a drug-free school.
You had better not bring drugs to campus, because this is a drug-free school.

(Collaborative option: Students work in pairs to discuss ways sentences could be rewritten.)

1. It was funny how Clem couldn't scarcely outrun the cops this time.

    _____

    _____

2. Just between you and I, he better get into shape before the marathon.

    _____

    _____

3. If and when they would have had kids, they would have been a lot happier.

    _____

    _____

4. They considered it okay for him to drive home, being that he had not drunk anything.

    _____

    _____

5. Irregardless of what the critics think, the new CD by the Mossy Stones will sell a half a million copies.

    _____

    _____

6. Clara was sort of hungry after them guests had eaten all her food.

    _____

    _____

7. Hopefully, this new tax will not impact on the poor an awful lot.

_____

_____

8. If he had of known that the authorities had contacted a bunch of his friends, he would of left town without waiting on a bus.

_____

_____

9. It being clear that everyone outside of John knew the truth, his friends planned on telling him.

_____

_____

10. They had seldom ever seen the manager so awful mad at anyone anywheres.

_____

_____

11. If Farley's appendix busts, there will be no doubt but that the family better rush him to a hospital.

_____

_____

12. The diplomats agreed that if they signed the treaty, you could be sure they'd avoid a confrontation in the Balkans.

_____

_____

13. "Aren't I lucky?" the woman exclaimed. She looked as if she couldn't help but bust with joy, being as how she had just won the lottery.

_____

_____

14. They had got an inkling that Raspley would try and foreclose the mortgage if and when the lovers married.

_____

_____

15. The generals read in the intelligence reports where the enemy forces had spread themselves every which way across the battlefront; plus, their troops must have been some fatigued after a couple days of forced marches.

_____

_____

_____

_____

73. WORD CHOICE: Nondiscriminatory Terms

(Study 403, Nondiscriminatory Terms)

Each sentence contains a sexist or other discriminatory term. **Circle** that term. Then, in the blank, write a nondiscriminatory replacement. (If the circled term should be deleted without a replacement, leave the line empty.)

Example: (Every citizen must use his) right to vote.

<u>All citizens must use their</u>

1. How I admire those brave pioneer men who brought civilization to the West!

2. Every student must bring his textbook to class.

3. All policemen are expected to be in full uniform while on duty.

4. Man's need to survive produces some surprising effects.

5. The speaker asserted that every gal in his audience should make her husband assume more household responsibilities.

6. The stewardess assured us that we would land in time for our connecting flight.

7. The female truck driver stopped and asked us for directions.

8. The innkeeper, his wife, and his children greeted us when we arrived at the inn.

9. The repairman's estimate was much lower than we had expected.

10. Everyone hoped that his or her proposal would be accepted.

_____

11. The spinster who lives upstairs never attends the block parties.

_____

12. The victim was shot by an unknown gunman.

_____

13. The new lady mathematics professor has published several textbooks.

_____

14. The college has a large ratio of Oriental students.

_____

15. The ecumenical worship service was open to all faiths, Christian and non-Christian.

_____

16. All kinds of persons with disabilities were there, including the mentally deficient.

_____

17. Our South Side neighborhood was home to many Italians and colored people.

_____

18. Why would you want to blacken your reputation by doing something like that?

_____

19. In our country people may attend whatever church they choose.

_____

20. Early in the fall the senior men began inviting girls to the graduation dance.

_____

74. WORD CHOICE: Similar Words Often Confused

(Study 404, Similar Words Often Confused)

Write the number of the **correct** choice.

Example: He sought his lawyer's (1)**advise** (2)**advice**.   _____2_____

1. Take my (1)**advice** (2)**advise**, Julius; stay home today.   1._____

2. If you (1)**break** (2)**brake** the car gently, you won't feel a jolt.   2._____

3. Camping trailers with (1)**canvas** (2)**canvass** tops are cooler than hardtop trailers.   3._____

4. The diamond tiara stolen from the museum exhibit weighed more than three (1)**carets** (2)**carats**.   4._____

5. The Dean of Student Affairs doubted whether the young man was a (1)**credible** (2)**creditable** witness to the fight in the dining hall.   5._____

6. Over the (1)**course** (2)**coarse** of the next month, the committee will review the sexual harassment policy.   6._____

7. Helping Allie with history was quite a (1)**descent** (2)**decent** gesture, don't you agree?   7._____

8. This little (1)**device** (2)**devise** will revolutionize the personal computer industry.   8._____

9. The professor made an (1)**illusion** (2)**allusion** to a recent disaster in Tokyo when describing crowd behavior.   9._____

10. She was one of the most (1)**eminent** (2)**imminent** educators of the decade.   10._____

11. We knew that enemy troops would try to (1)**envelop** (2)**envelope** us.   11._____

12. Go (1)**fourth** (2)**forth**, graduates, and be happy as well as successful.   12._____

13. Despite their obvious differences, the five students in Suite 401 had developed real friendship (1)**among** (2)**between** themselves.   13._____

14. The software game created by Frank really was (1)**ingenious** (2)**ingenuous**.   14._____

15. She tried vainly to (1)**lesson** (2)**lessen** the tension in the house.   15._____

16. The style of furniture is actually a matter of (1)**personal** (2)**personnel** taste.   16._____

17. Even though Gary studied hard and attended every class, he discovered that he was (1)**disinterested** (2)**uninterested** in majoring in chemistry.   17._____

18. The judge (1)**respectfully** (2)**respectively** called for the bailiff to read the jury's questions.   18._____

19. When the grand marshal gave the signal, the parade (1)**preceded** (2)**proceeded.**   19._____

20. Middle-aged professionals are forsaking their high-powered lifestyles for a (1)**quiet** (2)**quite** existence in the country.   20._____

21. (1)**Weather** (2)**Whether** to pay off all her creditors was a big question to be resolved.   21._____

22. We were so overweight that we bought a (1)**stationary** (2)**stationery** bicycle for our fifth anniversary.   22._____

23. The laser printer produces a much sharper image (1)**than** (2)**then** the older dot-matrix printer.   23._____

24. The computer operator read (1)**thorough** (2)**through** most of the manual before finding a possible solution.   24._____

25. The ability to pass doctoral qualifying exams is essentially a (1)**rite** (2)**right** of passage.　　25. _____

26. She is the first (1)**woman** (2)**women** to umpire in this league.　　26. _____

27. (1)**Your** (2)**You're** aware, aren't you, that the play is sold out?　　27. _____

28. This scanner will (1)**complement** (2)**compliment** your computer.　　28. _____

29. The student was (1)**anxious** (2)**eager** to receive his award at the banquet.　　29. _____

30. It will take me (1)**awhile** (2)**a while** to finish these calculations.　　30. _____

31. The best advice is to take a long walk if you (1)**lose** (2)**loose** your temper.　　31. _____

32. Some of the television programs needed to be (1)**censored** (2)**censured** by parents because they were showing extreme violence before 9 p.m.　　32. _____

33. Nobody (1)**accept** (2)**except** Gloria would stoop so low.　　33. _____

34. Sam unplugged his phone, locked his door, and worked (1)**continuously** (2)**continually** on his research paper.　　34. _____

35. Her approach for preparing for the history final was (1)**different from** (2)**different than** my strategy.　　35. _____

36. (1)**Everyone** (2)**Every one** of the computers was destroyed by the flood.　　36. _____

37. If John (1)**passed** (2)**past** the physics final, it must have been easy.　　37. _____

38. The library copy of the magazine had lost (1)**its** (2)**it's** cover.　　38. _____

39. For (1)**instance,** (2)**instants,** this computer doesn't have enough memory to run that particular word-processing package.　　39. _____

40. The firm is (1)**already** (2)**all ready** for any negative publicity from the outcome of the lawsuit.　　40. _____

41. Can you name the (1)**capitals** (2)**capitols** of all fifty states?　　41. _____

42. His physical condition showed the (1)**affects** (2)**effects** of inadequate rest and diet.　　42. _____

43. My gregarious little niece was (1)**eager** (2)**anxious** to go to the party.　　43. _____

44. Shall we dress (1)**formally** (2)**formerly** for the Senior Ball?　　44. _____

45. To be an effective teacher had become her (1)**principal** (2)**principle** concern.　　45. _____

46. More than a million people (1)**emigrated** (2)**immigrated** from Ireland during the nineteenth-century potato famine.　　46. _____

47. The Farkle family were (1)**altogether** (2)**all together** in the living room when the grandmother announced that she was willing her money to a nearby cat sanctuary.　　47. _____

48. The student (1)**inferred** (2)**implied** from the professor's expression that the final exam would be challenging.　　48. _____

49. "I, (1)**to** (2)**too** (3)**two**, have a statement to make," she said.　　49. _____

50. Homelessness—(1)**its** (2)**it's** no longer just an American problem.　　50. _____

75. WORD CHOICE: Similar Words Often Confused

(Study 404, Similar Words Often Confused)

Write the number of the **correct** choice.

Example: He sought his lawyer's (1)**advise** (2)**advice**.   _____2_____

1. Chris feels (1)**good** (2)**well** about the results of the faculty survey.   1._____

2. He said, "(1)**Their** (2)**There** (3)**They're** is no reason for you to wait."   2._____

3. "(1)**Whose** (2)**Who's** there?" she whispered.   3._____

4. The cat ran behind my car, and I accidentally ran over (1)**its** (2)**it's** tail.   4._____

5. The consultant will (1)**ensure** (2)**insure** that the audit is completed on time.   5._____

6. The twins (1)**formally** (2)**formerly** attended a private college in California.   6._____

7. The mere (1)**cite** (2)**site** (3)**sight** of Julia made his heart soar.   7._____

8. Will people be standing in the (1)**aisles** (2)**isles** at the dedication ceremony?   8._____

9. Dr. Smith is (1)**famous** (2)**notorious** for her educational research.   9._____

10. "Sad movies always (1)**affect** (2)**effect** me that way," lamented Kay.   10._____

11. The (1)**thorough** (2)**through** commission report indicated that approximately forty percent of American schools do not have enough textbooks in their classrooms.   11._____

12. Jonathon had the (1)**presence** (2)**presents** of mind to make a sharp right turn and to step on the accelerator.   12._____

13. The principal expected the students' behavior to (1)**correspond to** (2)**correspond with** the school district's expectations.   13._____

14. If you rehearse enough, you're (1)**likely** (2)**liable** to get the lead role in the play.   14._____

15. The family has (1)**born** (2)**borne** the noise and dust of the nearby highway construction for several months.   15._____

16. (1)**Their** (2)**They're** (3)**There** leasing a truck because they can't afford the down payment to purchase a new one.   16._____

17. The time capsule (1)**may be** (2)**maybe** the best way for the general public to understand how people lived one hundred years ago.   17._____

18. Some (1)**individual** (2)**person** dropped off a package at the mailroom.   18._____

19. The track coach told me that he wanted to (1)**discuss** (2)**discus** my performance at the last meet.   19._____

20. The voters are (1)**apt** (2)**likely** to vote for a candidate who promises to reduce unemployment.   20._____

21. (1)**Who's** (2)**Whose** theory do you believe regarding the geographical origin of humankind?   21._____

22. The (1)**council** (2)**counsel** (3)**consul** met to decide the fate of the student who cheated on the psychology final.   22._____

23. A tall tree has fallen and is (1)**laying** (2)**lying** across the highway.   23._____

24. A significant (1)**percent** (2)**percentage** of Americans still smoke.   24._____

25. In *The Oxbow Incident*, the wrong man is (1)**hung** (2)**hanged**.   25._____

26. Did you ask if he will (1)**let** (2)**leave** you open a charge account?   26. _____

27. The new dance had (1)**to** (2)**too** (3)**two** many steps to remember.   27. _____

28. Sarah promised to (1)**learn** (2)**teach** me some gardening techniques.   28. _____

29. Shooting innocent bystanders is one of the most (1)**amoral** (2)**immoral** street crimes committed.   29. _____

30. The alfalfa milkshake may taste unpleasant, but it is (1)**healthy** (2)**healthful**.   30. _____

31. The tennis player always (1)**lays** (2)**lies** down before an important match.   31. _____

32. When (1)**your** (2)**you're** in love, the whole world seems beautiful.   32. _____

33. On high school basketball courts Sam was often (1)**compared to** (2)**compared with** the young Michael Jordan.   33. _____

34. The (1)**amount** (2)**number** of trees needed to produce a single book should humble any author.   34. _____

35. This medication will (1)**lessen** (2)**lesson** the pain until we reach the emergency room.   35. _____

36. The newspaper was soggy because it had (1)**laid** (2)**lain** in a rain puddle all morning.   36. _____

37. After spending $1,000 on repairs, we hope that the van finally works (1)**like** (2)**as** it should.   37. _____

38. The couple (1)**adapted** (2)**adopted** a baby girl from Bulgaria.   38. _____

39. Cindy was (1)**besides** (2)**beside** herself with anger.   39. _____

40. The agreement was (1)**among** (2)**between** Harry and me.   40. _____

41. Do not (1)**set** (2)**sit** the floppy disk on top of the computer monitor.   41. _____

42. The play was from (1)**classical** (2)**classic** Rome.   42. _____

43. The curtain was about to (1)**raise** (2)**rise** on the last act of the senior play.   43. _____

44. The camp is just a few miles (1)**farther** (2)**further** along the trail.   44. _____

45. The news report (1)**convinced** (2)**persuaded** me to join a volunteer organization that renovates homes in low-income neighborhoods.   45. _____

46. The author of that particular book was (1)**censored** (2)**censured** for his views by a national parenting group.   46. _____

47. You may borrow (1)**any one** (2)**anyone** of my books if you promise to return it.   47. _____

48. Compared (1)**to** (2)**with** the Steelers, the Raiders have a weaker defense but a stronger offense.   48. _____

49. The linebacking unit was (1)**composed** (2)**comprised** of Taylor, Marshall, and Burt.   49. _____

50. The three children tried to outrun (1)**each other** (2)**one another**.   50. _____

76. WORD CHOICE: Review

(Study 401–404, Word Choice)

Each sentence may contain an inappropriate or incorrect expression. **Circle** that expression, and in the blank write an appropriate or correct replacement. Use standard, formal American English. If the sentence is correct as is, leave the blank empty.

Examples: He sought his lawyer's (advise.)____advice____

The director reported that the company (was fine and dandy.)____had doubled its profits.____

Whose idea was it? _____

1. Those sort of books are expensive. _____

2. The cabin was just like I remembered it from childhood vacations. _____

3. Some children look like their parents. _____

4. I was surprised that the banquet was attended by lots of people. _____

5. Its time for class. _____

6. You too can afford such a car. _____

7. I can't hardly hear the speaker. _____

8. Randy promised me that he is over with being angry with me. _____

9. Irregardless of the result, you did your best. _____

10. Will he raise your salary? _____

11. Try to keep him off of the pier. _____

12. I usually always stop at this corner meat market when I am having dinner guests. _____

13. You are selling vanilla, chocolate, and black cherry? I'll take the latter. _____

14. His efforts at improving communication among all fifty staff members will determine his own success. _____

15. Her success was due to hard work and persistence. _____

16. I'm invited, aren't I? _____

17. Their house is now for sale. _____

18. Henry and myself decided to start a small business together. _____

19. The club lost its president. _____

20. Did he lay awake last night? _____

21. The professor's opinion differed with the teaching assistant's perspective. _____

22. Bob laid the carpet in the hallway. _____

23. The cat has been laying on top of the refrigerator all morning.

    _____

24. He has plenty of opportunities for earning money. _____

25. San Francisco offers many things for tourists to do. _____

26. Most all her friends are married. _____

27. He always did good in English courses. _____

28. The low price of the printer plus the modem prompted me to buy both.

    _____

29. Because her supervisor seemed unreasonable, Sue finally decided to resign.

    _____

30. Max has less enemies than Sam. _____

31. The speaker inferred that time management depended more on attitude than skill.

    _____

32. Glenn has a long way to travel each week. _____

33. Did he loose his wallet and credit cards? _____

34. She looked like she was afraid. _____

35. Walking to school was a rite of passage in our home.

    _____

36. Who were the principals in the company? _____

37. Have you written in regards to an appointment? _____

38. Elaine adopted her novel for television. _____

39. Damp weather affects her sinuses. _____

40. A lion hunting its prey is immoral. _____

41. The troop was already to leave for camp. _____

42. The men and girls on the team played well. _____

43. We split the bill between the three of us. _____

44. Be sure to wear causal clothes to tonight's party.

    _____

45. The hum of the air conditioner was continual. _____

46. The informer was hanged. _____

47. The air conditioner runs good now. _____

48. The child is too young to understand. _____

49. Regardless of his shortcomings, she loves him. _____

50. Where is the party at? _____

51. Please bring these plans to the engineering department. _____ _____

52. The salesman was looking forward to the sale. _____

53. The sun will hopefully shine today. _____

54. Their political strategy failed in the end. _____

55. The workmen complained that the work site was unsafe.
_____

56. His chances for a promotion looked good. _____

57. The twins frequently wear one another's clothing. _____

58. A twisted branch was laying across our path. _____

59. She was disinterested in the boring play. _____

60. Send a cover letter to the chair of the department. _____

61. This line is for shoppers with ten items or fewer. _____

62. The hostile countries finally effected a compromise.
_____

63. The professor was somewhat annoyed at the girls in his class.
_____

64. Sam differed from Gina about the issue of increasing social services.
_____

65. I meant to lay down for just an hour. _____

66. Let us think further about it. _____

67. He is the most credible person I have ever met. He will believe anything.
_____

68. He enjoys the healthy food we serve. _____

69. Paul's conversation was sprinkled with literary illusions.
_____

70. The husband and wife were both pursuing law degrees.
_____

71. Her position in the company was most unique. _____

72. He has already departed. _____

73. I will have to rite a letter to that company. _____

74. There's was an informal agreement. _____

75. Durnell is a student which always puts his studies first.
_____

76. Their is always another game. _____

77. The gold locket had lain on the floor of the attic for ten years.
_____

78. Foyt lead the race from start to finish. _____

79. By the tone of her writing, the news reporter implied that the politician was guilty of fraud.
_____

80. To find the missing watch, we ventured further into the crowd.
_____

77. WORD CHOICE: Review

(Study 401–404, Word Choice)

On your own paper, **rewrite** each paragraph below so that it displays all the word-choice skills you have learned, but none of the word-choice faults you have been cautioned against. Use standard, formal English.

(Collaborative option: Students work in pairs or small groups to discuss each paragraph, suggest new wording, and edit one another's work.)

1. It has been brought to our attention that company personnel have been engaging in the taking of unauthorized absences from their daily stations. The affect of this action is to leave these stations laying unattended for durations of time extending up to a quarter of an hour. In this day and age such activity is inexcusable. Therefore the management has reached the conclusion that tried and true disciplinary measures must necessarily be put into effect. Thus, commencing August 5, workmen who render theirselves absent from their work station will have a certain amount of dollars deducted from the wages they are paid.

2.   Needless Required College Courses [title of essay]

    The topic of which I shall write about in this paper is needless required college courses. I will show in the following paragraphs that many mandatory required courses are really unnecessary. They have no purpose due to the fact that they are not really needed or wanted but exist just to provide jobs for professors which cannot attract students by themselfs on there own. It is this that makes them meaningless.

3. In my opinion, I think that the general consensus of opinion is usually always that the reason why lots of people fail to engage in the voting procedure is because they would rather set around home then get off of they're tails and get down to the nearest voting facility. In regards to this matter some things ought to be done to get an O.K. percent of the American people to vote.

4. Each and every day we learn, verbally or from newspapers, about business executives having heart attacks and every so often ending up dead. The stress of high management-type positions is said to be the principle casual factor in such attacks. But a search threw available data shows that this is a unfounded belief. For awhile it was universally expected that persons in high-level jobs experienced the most stress. But yet this is such a misconception. It is in the low-echelon jobs that more strain and consequently more heart attacks occur.

5. The Bible's Book of Exodus relates the flight of the ancient Jews from Egypt to Israel. The narrative says where God sent ten plagues upon the land, the reason why being to punish the rulers for not letting the Jewish people go. Moses then lead his people across the Red Sea, who's waves parted to leave them go through. There trek thorough the desert lasted weaks, months, and than years. The people's moral began to sag. However, Moses brought them the Ten Commandments from Mt. Sinai, and they emigrated safely into the Promised Land. Moses, though, died before he could enter this very fine country. Some question the historic accuracy of the narrative, but others find it entirely credulous. If you except it fully or not, its one of the world's most engrossing stories.

78. PARAGRAPHS AND PAPERS: Topic Sentences and Paragraph Unity

(Study 503A, The Topic Sentence, and 503D, Unity and Emphasis)

First, **circle** the topic sentence of each paragraph. Then find one or more sentences that violate the **unity** of the paragraph (that do not relate directly to the topic). Write the number(s) of the sentence(s) in the blank at the end of the paragraph.

1. (1)From a pebble on the shore to a boulder on a mountainside, any rock you see began as something else and was made a rock by the earth itself. (2)Igneous rock began as lava that over hundreds of years hardened far beneath the earth's surface. (3)Granite is an igneous rock that is very hard and used for buildings and monuments. (4)Sedimentary rock was once sand, mud, or clay that settled to the bottom of a body of water and was packed down in layers under the ocean floor. (5)All rocks are made up of one or more minerals. (6)Metamorphic rock began as either igneous rock or sedimentary rock whose properties were changed by millions of years of exposure to the heat, pressure, and movement below the earth's crust.

   1. _____

2. (1)Although we normally associate suits of armor with the knights of medieval Europe, the idea of such protective coverings is much older and more pervasive than that. (2)Some knights even outfitted their horses with metal armor. (3)As long as 3,500 years ago, Assyrian and Babylonian warriors sewed pieces of metal to their leather tunics the better to repel enemy arrows. (4)A thousand years later, the Greeks wore metal helmets, in addition to large metal sheets over their chests and backs. (5)Native Americans of the Northwest wore both carved wooden helmets and chest armor made from wood and leather. (6)Nature protects the turtle and the armadillo with permanent armor. (7)Even with body armor largely absent from the modern soldier's uniform, the helmet still remains as a reminder of the vulnerability of the human body.

   2. _____

3. (1)Mention the name of George Washington and most Americans envision a larger-than-life hero, who, even as a little boy, could not tell a lie. (2)However, it turns out that Washington was more human than his biographers would have us believe. (3)His contemporaries described Washington as moody and remote. (4)He was also a bit vain, for he insisted that his fellow officers address him as "Your Excellency." (5)He refused to allow himself to be touched by strangers. (6)Washington was also known to weep in public, especially when the Patriots' war effort was sagging. (7)Washington was even plagued with traitors, who gave the British advice on how to beat the Americans. (8)He was not even a gifted military officer. (9)Rather than being a hero of the French and Indian War, Washington may have provoked the French to go to war by leading an unnecessary and irrational attack against a group of Frenchmen. (10)While Washington was certainly a brave man, dedicated to freeing the colonists from British tyranny, he was not the perfect man that early biographers described.

   3. _____

4. (1)In the mid-1800s, an apple or a pear was considered too dangerous to eat. (2)In fact, any fresh vegetable or fruit was considered too risky because one bite might lead to cholera, dysentery, or typhoid. (3)During cholera epidemics, city councils often banned the sale of fruits and vegetables. (4)The only safe vegetable was a boiled potato. (5)A typical breakfast might include black tea, scrambled eggs, fresh spring shad, wild pigeons, pig's feet, and oysters. (6)Milk was also considered a perilous beverage because many people died from drinking spoiled milk. (7)Milk really was a threat to people's health, because it was processed and delivered to home with little regard for hygiene. (8)Children and those who were ill were often malnourished because the foods with the most nutrients were also the most deadly. (9)Until the invention of the icebox in the 1840s, rich and poor people alike risked their health and even their lives every time they ate a meal.

4. _____

5. (1)Infant sacrifice must be clearly differentiated from infanticide. (2)The latter practice, growing out of economic want, was not uncommon among primitive peoples whose food supply was inadequate. (3)Even in most of the Greek city-states, in Rome, and among the Norsemen before they accepted Christianity, it was the father's right to determine whether his newborn child should be accepted and nurtured or instead be abandoned—simply left to perish from exposure. (4)In the eighth and ninth centuries the Norse invaded Britain and left elements of their linguistic and cultural heritage. (5)But in infant sacrifice a father offered this most precious gift to the gods. (6)Thus Abraham was told: "Take now thy son, thine only son Isaac, whom thou lovest, and get thee into the land of Moriah; and offer him there for a burnt offering upon one of the mountains, which I will tell thee of."

—Constance Irwin (adapted)

5. _____

79. PARAGRAPHS AND PAPERS: Paragraph Development

(Study 503B, Adequate Development)

Each paragraph below is inadequately developed. Choose **one**, and, on the back of this page or on your own paper, **rewrite** it to develop the topic sentence (boldfaced) adequately. Use six to nine sentences, adding your own facts and ideas as needed. (You may change the topic sentence to express a different viewpoint.)

(Collaborative option: Students work in pairs or small groups to pool information, discuss how to develop paragraphs, and review or edit one another's work.)

1. Young people today see how their parents act and how they feel about the world today. Since they feel their parents are wrong, they rebel because they do not want to become a carbon copy of their elders. Young people want to be treated as persons, not just kids who do not know what they are talking about and who should not express their own ideas because they are too young to understand. **Young people today want to do and think as they please.**

2. **Traffic is choking our community.** Every morning and evening at rush hour the streets are clogged with commuters' cars. There are just too many of them. I see this every weekday. And on weekends the roads to nearby resorts are almost as crowded. This problem is ruining our community, and something must be done about it.

3. **I like the old movies shown on TV better than the recent releases shown in theaters.** The old films contain more-dramatic plots and more-famous actors. They are exciting and fast paced. The actors are widely known for their acting ability. Today's films are boring or mindless and have less-famous actors.

80. PARAGRAPHS AND PAPERS: Paragraph Coherence

(Study 503C, Coherence)

In each blank, write the transitional expression from the list below that fits most logically. For some blanks there is more than one correct answer. Try not to use any expression more than once.

afterward	meanwhile	more important	however
consequently	nevertheless	therefore	likewise
even so	on the other hand	thus	in particular
formerly	finally	as a result	that is

Example: Thousands of workers were heading home by car, bus, and train. <u>Meanwhile,</u> at home, their spouses were readying supper.

1. The rescue workers searched for victims in the debris for more than twelve hours until relieved; _____, as they sat and wearily sipped coffee, they vented their frustration at finding no survivors.

2. Arthur, in Jacksonville, was trying frantically to call Rachel about the news; _____, in Sacramento, Rachel was desperately trying to reach him.

3. Today we take a common United States currency for granted. Money, _____, was not standardized in the U.S. until the Civil War, when the federal government produced its first paper money.

4. In postwar America people were enjoying a strong economy, which provided plenty of jobs and high wages; _____, life seemed secure and promising.

5. The term *teenager* entered the language only as recently as 1941; _____, teenagers were not really a recognized presence in American society.

6. When we speak to family members, we use an informal and intimate language. When we are speaking to a large group, _____, we are more likely to choose different words and a different tone of voice.

7. If you toss a coin repeatedly and it comes up heads each time, common sense tells you to expect tails to turn up soon. _____, the chances of heads coming up remain the same for each toss of the coin.

8. The first real movie—_____, one that actually had a story line—was the film entitled *The Great Train Robbery.*

9. American children spend about a quarter of their waking time watching television; _____, it is important to monitor what young children are watching.

10. A seven-hundred pound microwave oven, called the Radarange, was first produced by Tappan in 1955. _____, Americans were not interested in purchasing a microwave oven until the late 1960s, when the appliance was much smaller and more reliable.

11. The young singing group tried again and again to produce a hit recording, without success; _____, they struck gold with "Gotta Have Your Love."

12. Whelan's stocks soared 350 points in a day; _____, she felt that she could buy an expensive new car.

13. Some baseball records have been thought unbreakable; _____, few people expected Lou Gehrig's 2,130-consecutive-game streak ever to fall.

14. Nineteen forty-one marked the beginning of Franklin Roosevelt's third term; _____, it was the year that the U.S. was plunged into World War II.

81. PARAGRAPHS AND PAPERS: Paragraph Review, Netiquette

(Study 503C, Coherence, and 504, Netiquette)

Part 1

Go back to the paragraph you wrote in exercise 79.

On your own paper or in the space below, **rewrite** it, being sure that it has a controlling structure, appropriate transitions, and repeated key words or phrases as needed to give it coherence. **Circle** your transitions and repeated key words or phrases. At the end, skip a line and **write a sentence** briefly stating what your controlling structure is.

(Collaborative option: Students work in pairs or small groups to assist one another in revising.)

A student sent the following e-mail in response to an online job offer. On the lines below, **rewrite** the e-mail in appropriate English, changing, deleting or adding text as necessary. (This is a preliminary contact, not a full application letter.)

FROM: Pat Benson

TO: Online Services Company

SUBJECT: Your Website

DATE: October 18, 2005

Hi there!

I got real enthused when I saw your job offer on your Website August 5. In this day and age you won't find many as UNIQUE as me. Being as how I have taken a lot of computer courses and plan on taking more, I can, IMHO, handle ANY THING I could meet up with in your service department. If you can utilize my services, contact me. I'll be waiting anxiously. Gotta go now. Bye! ☺

Pat

FROM: _____

TO: _____

SUBJECT: _____

DATE: _____

_____

_____

_____

_____

_____

_____

_____

_____

_____

_____

_____

_____

_____

_____

_____

_____

_____

_____

82. PARAGRAPHS AND PAPERS: The Thesis Sentence

(Study 505C, Forming a Thesis)

First, from the list below, **identify** the main weakness in each thesis sentence, and write the letter of that weakness in the short blank. Then, in the long blanks, **rewrite** the thesis sentence so that it is usable for an essay. (For the purposes of this exercise, you may invent facts or ideas as needed.)

A–no assertion   C–too broad, too vague, or unsupportable
B–split focus   D–stale, uninteresting to U.S. collegians

Examples: Our nation's social problems need solving now.   _____C_____
Our college has a moral obligation to use part of its endowment to relieve local poverty.

The Antarctic is one of the coldest places on earth.   _____A_____
Despite its inhospitable climate, new scientific advances hold promise for making the
Antarctic a desirable place for people to live.

(Collaborative option: Students work in pairs or small groups to evaluate thesis sentences and compose new ones.)

1. Canada is actually larger than the United States.   1. _____

2. Radio can be more entertaining than television, and radio commercials are more profitable for sponsors than those on TV.   2. _____

3. Spring is a lovely time of year.   3. _____

4. Studying the types of sand in Mongolia's Gobi Desert can be rewarding.   4. _____

5. A drug experience really affects a person.   5. _____

6. The state's welfare system is inhumane, and its housing rehabilitation program is in shambles.   6. _____

_____

_____

7. I experienced the birth of twins.   7. _____

_____

_____

8. I have strong feelings about euthanasia.   8. _____

_____

_____

9. Air pollution will kill off the human race.   9. _____

_____

_____

10. The scourge of acne must be eliminated.   10. _____

_____

_____

83. PARAGRAPHS AND PAPERS: Planning the Essay

(Study 505A–D, Before Starting to Write)

Follow the directions below.

_____

(Collaborative option: Students work in pairs or small groups to share knowledge and ideas and to offer suggestions.)

A. Assume that you have been assigned to write an essay in one of these broad subject areas: popular music, man-woman relationships, improving this college. Choose one. On your own paper, **brainstorm, freewrite,** or **cluster** whatever ideas you can generate on this subject. From those ideas, produce **three** limited topics suitable for a 2- to 4-page essay. List those topics here:

1._____

2._____

3._____

B. From each of these topics, develop the best tentative thesis sentence you can for this 2- to 4-page essay:

Topic 1:_____

_____

Topic 2:_____

_____

Topic 3:_____

_____

From these three, choose the one that, considering your knowledge, ideas, and interests, you can best develop into an essay. Refine that thesis sentence and write it here:

Topic #____: _____

_____

C. Consider which approach seems most workable for this topic and thesis: narration, description, explanation, persuasion, problem-solution, effect-cause (or vice versa), comparison/contrast. State your most likely approach:

_____

D. List below the major divisions (subtopics) you see for your essay (three is the most common number, but others may work better for your topic). If you chose the persuasive approach, for example, each division would probably be a separate reason.

Divisions:

_____

_____

_____

_____

84. PARAGRAPHS AND PAPERS: The Essay Outline

(Study 505E, Outlining)

In the space below, write a detailed **outline** for the essay you began preparing in exercise 83. Continue on the back or on your own paper if necessary. Use any of the methods mentioned in section 505E. Make it detailed enough so that you can write an essay from it.

(Collaborative option: Students work in pairs or small groups to construct the outline or evaluate one another's outlines.)

85. PARAGRAPHS AND PAPERS: The Essay Introduction and Conclusion

(Study 506, Writing and Revising the Essay; Review 502–503, Paragraphs)

Part 1

Each sentence is the opening of an essay. In the blank, write **Y** (for **yes**) if the sentence is an **effective interest-arouser**. Write **N** (for **no**) if it is **not**.

Example: The United States faces many problems today.   _____N_____

(Collaborative option: Students in pairs or small groups discuss the effectiveness of each sentence.)

1. Throughout my life I have encountered many interesting situations and experiences.   1. _____

2. It is 7 a.m. this bitter cold December day, and the line outside the employment agency has grown bigger since I arrived at 5.   2. _____

3. There are many things that bring a person joy in life, and many things that bring sadness.   3. _____

4. One of the biggest-selling items in this city's public housing project supermarkets is dog food—yet no dogs are allowed in the projects.   4. _____

5. In the past few years Americans generally have lost interest in threats from global warming and the ozone hole, yet both are still on the increase and no one is sounding the alarm.   5. _____

6. The United States is a very different place from what it was a hundred years ago, or even fifty, all because of different circumstances that have surrounded people in each era.   6. _____

7. What would you do if your life savings were suddenly wiped out and you and all your family lost their jobs, as happened to our great-grandparents in the Depression?   7. _____

8. Our hike that day started just like many others we had taken through the Appalachians, until we stepped around a fallen tree and recoiled in horror.   8. _____

9. The figures are awesome: a world population today of more than 6 billion, with more than a million newcomers every week.   9. _____

10. In my short but checkered career I have worked at a wide variety of jobs, some indoors and some out, some easy and some hard.   10. _____

Part 2

Each item contains the closing sentence(s) of an essay. In the blank, write **Y** (for **yes**) if the sentence is an **effective closing**. Write **N** (for **no**) if it is **not**.

Example: And so we must do something about this problem.   _____N_____

(Collaborative option: Students in pairs or small groups discuss the effectiveness of each sentence.)

1. On the whole, as I said before, my experience was one of the many things I remember as significant in my life.   1. _____

2. I can still remember how I felt as I stood there with all those people looking at me while I had to pay my restaurant bill with borrowed nickels and dimes.   2. _____

3. The dining hall in which we must all eat, and to whose employees we must entrust our health, is, as I have shown, a pigsty. The time has come to start doing something about it.

3. _____

4. This experience changed my whole attitude toward money, making me ruthlessly determined never again to be embarrassed by lack of funds. We all seem to suffer more from such humiliations than from any other kind of defeat, even a physical beating, a job lost, or a romance gone sour. Along with hunger and sex, the fear of looking bad in the eyes of others is one of the most basic of human motives.

4. _____

5. Therefore, every citizen should go to the polls this election day and vote for Maryann Rivera for governor. Another reason is that her opponent is old and may die in office.

5. _____

6. The federal government, then, must cut the money supply before it is too late; otherwise, as in Germany in the 1920s, our money may literally not be worth the paper on which it is printed.

6. _____

7. Every spring since that day my parents first took me to Wrigley Field, my heart pounds with anticipation when I hear the cry "Play ball!" Keep your football, basketball, and hockey; baseball will always be America's game.

7. _____

8. Thus, since there are more people in the world today than can be fed, and a million more arriving weekly, it is up to the United Nations to take the bull by the horns and find a solution to the problem.

8. _____

9. Since poverty will never disappear, it is up to leaders of the prosperous nations, particularly the United States, to shift their focus from assuring middle-class comfort to making laws and programs that will create a vast new Marshall Plan to feed the hungry at home and worldwide. Perhaps then those in our housing projects will not have to subsist on dog food.

9. _____

10. [For this item, supply your own effective conclusion.]
I, then, am one of those who have grown up as so-called victims of society. _____

_____

_____

_____

Part 3

On your own paper: First, write an effective **introductory paragraph** for the essay you outlined in exercise 84. Then write an effective **concluding paragraph** for the same essay. (These may be considered drafts until you complete exercise 86. Or your instructor may have you defer writing the conclusion until you have completed exercise 86.)

_____

(Collaborative option: Students in pairs or small groups critique one another's paragraphs.)

86. PARAGRAPHS AND PAPERS: The Essay Body

(Study 506, Writing and Revising the Essay; Review 502–503, Paragraphs)

Part 1

In the blanks, write an effective **topic sentence** for each body paragraph of the essay you have been planning and writing in exercises 83, 84, and 85. (You do not have to use all five sets of blanks; use as many body paragraphs as the structure of your essay demands.) Include a transitional expression or sentence that links each paragraph to the preceding one.

Example: At first, in the late 1970s and early '80s, personal computers were incredibly primitive by today's standards.

(Collaborative option: Students in pairs or small groups discuss the effectiveness of each sentence.)

1. _____

   _____

   _____

2. _____

   _____

   _____

3. _____

   _____

   _____

4. _____

   _____

   _____

5. _____

   _____

   _____

Part 2

On your own paper, complete the **body paragraphs** of your essay. Remember what section 503B stated about supporting evidence.

(Collaborative option: Students in pairs or small groups critique one another's work.)

Part 3

Bring your introductory, body, and concluding paragraphs together. On your own paper, **revise**, **edit**, and **proofread** your essay until you are satisfied with its quality. Submit a clean copy.

(Collaborative option: Students in pairs or small groups critique, edit, and proofread one another's work.)

87. PARAGRAPHS AND PAPERS: Research Paper Topics and Theses

(Study 507A, Choosing and Limiting a Topic, and 507B, Forming a Thesis)

Part 1

If the topic is **suitable** for a research paper, write **Y** (for **Yes**) in the blank. If the topic is **not suitable**, write the **letter of the reason** in the blank. (For some items there is more than one possible correct answer.)

A—too broad, vague, or speculative
B—not researchable or completable with available resources
C—unable to be treated objectively

Example: Poland's transition from communism to capitalism, 1985–1995 _____Y_____

1. Muslim-Christian conflicts since the year 1000   1. _____
2. Is there intelligent life in our solar system?   2. _____
3. Attitudes toward wealth in F. Scott Fitzgerald's story "The Rich Boy"   3. _____
4. The coming triumph of feminism   4. _____
5. The torch is passed: the effects of the 1960 presidential election on the Cold War   5. _____
6. Symbols in the writings of Willa Cather   6. _____
7. New treatments of athletic knee injuries in girls and women   7. _____
8. Devil worship: the one true religion   8. _____
9. Voting patterns of current freshmen at this college in public elections   9. _____
10. The collapse of communism as seen through the eyes of selected average Russians   10. _____
11. The ruination of America's moral standards through unrestricted use of the Internet   11. _____
12. The decline in foreign trade as a cause of the Great Depression   12. _____
13. The Great Depression: it could happen again   13. _____
14. The interstate highway system in our state, 1955–1975: boon or boondoggle?   14. _____

Part 2

In the short blank, write **Y** (for **yes**) if the thesis sentence is a **workable** one for a research paper. Write **N** (for **no**) if it is **not**. Then, after each sentence for which you wrote **N**, write in the long blank a workable thesis sentence on the same topic.

Example: Roosevelt's China policy before World War II was bad.   _____N_____
              Roosevelt's China policy helped draw the U.S. into World War II.

(Collaborative option: Students in pairs or small groups suggest workable thesis sentences.)

1. F. Scott Fitzgerald, in his story "The Rich Boy," conveys ambivalent attitudes toward wealth.   1. _____

   _____

   _____

   _____

2. The U.S. election of 1960 radically changed the history of the world.   2. _____

   _____

   _____

   _____

3. Throughout *Huckleberry Finn*, the Mississippi River can be seen as Mark Twain's symbol for life and freedom.   3. _____

   _____

   _____

   _____

4. The lost continent of Atlantis lies just off the sea in the Bermuda Triangle, waiting to be discovered.   4. _____

   _____

   _____

   _____

5. The Second Vatican Council played only a secondary role in the widespread defection of U.S. Catholics in the 1960s and '70s.   5. _____

   _____

   _____

   _____

6. Despite being maligned by critics, current afternoon TV talk shows tend to raise the cultural level of all their viewers.   6. _____

   _____

   _____

   _____

7. The present family court system in this county often harms the very people it is intended to help.   7. _____

   _____

   _____

   _____

8. The U.S. Electoral College should be replaced by direct popular vote because the College system distorts vote totals.

8. _____

_____

_____

_____

9. Shakespeare's works really had to have been written by Francis Bacon because Bacon was educated and Shakespeare was not.

9. _____

_____

_____

_____

10. Devil worship has grown in the U.S. in recent years primarily because of its appeal to alienated youth.

10. _____

_____

_____

_____

11. Massive urban renewal projects in the 1960s and 1970s failed throughout the nation; I know because I grew up in one of them.

11. _____

_____

_____

_____

88. PARAGRAPHS AND PAPERS: Locating and Evaluating Sources

(Study 507C and E, Locating and Evaluating Sources, and 509, Works Cited/References)

Part 1

Choose one of the subjects below. In the library, **locate** five useful printed (not electronic) sources on your subject. In the space on this page, **list** the needed bibliographical information for each, in either **MLA** or **APA** form (or the **COS** alternative for either), as your instructor directs. (For books, also make a note of the call number.)

U.S. responses to the al-Qaeda
   threat before September 11, 2001
Honky-tonk music
The relation of dinosaurs to birds

U.S. national parks since 1950
U.S. automobile safety since 1950
F. Scott Fitzgerald's early short stories
   (up to 1925)

(Collaborative option: Students in pairs or small groups share research tasks and findings.)

Follow the directions for part 1, using the same topic you chose there. This time use electronic instead of printed sources. Be sure to include Internet addresses or other needed information for retrieval, where necessary.

Evaluate the usability of each of the following sources for a research paper titled "The Choosing of U.S. Vice-presidential Candidates, 1980–2000." In the blank, write the number of your evaluation:

1—source is unquestionably usable

2—source is usable but needs to be balanced with a source giving a different viewpoint

3—source is not usable

Example: A 1982 pamphlet urging people to boycott the election   3

1. The *Congressional Record*, published regularly by the U.S. Congress, including speeches of several future Vice-presidents   1. _____

2. Your parent's high school American history textbook   2. _____

3. A Pulitzer Prize-winning book by a noted historian, on the American Vice-presidency, published in 2001   3. _____

4. An article, "A Day with the Vice-president," in the current issue of a magazine sold at your supermarket checkout   4. _____

5. An article on the 1986 election in the *Journal of Political Science*   5. _____

6. A Web site sponsored by the Republican National Committee   6. _____

7. A book, *The American Vice-presidency*, published by Harvard University Press in 1993   7. _____

8. An e-mail from a friend who is a Washington intern in the Vice-president's secretary's office   8. _____

9. A 1996 article in the *Nation* magazine, titled "A Liberal's-eye View of Recent Vice-presidents"   9. _____

10. A Web site named "Traitorous Capitalist Pigs in the White House"   10. _____

89. PARAGRAPHS AND PAPERS: Taking Notes, Citing, Avoiding Plagiarism

(Study 507F, Taking Notes; 508A, Citing Within the Paper; and 508B, Avoiding Plagiarism)*

Part 1

Each item below contains an original passage from a source, followed by a student's note card on the passage. The student has done one or more of the following:

(1) incorrectly or inadequately keyed the note card to its corresponding bibliography card,

(2) misrepresented or distorted what the source said,

(3) come too close to the source's wording (plagiarized).

In the blank note card, **write** a correctly keyed, accurate, unplagiarized note on the passage.

Example: [From page 197 of a book by Antonia Fraser called *The Wives of Henry VIII*. (Catherine is the former Queen; Henry's new Queen is Anne.)]

ORIGINAL: Meanwhile at the court these days, there were indications to encourage Catherine's supporters that all was not well between the King and the new Queen.

STUDENT:

```
Wives of Hen. 8th–197

At this time in the palace, indications
encouraged Catherine's supporters that
things were not well between the King and
his new Queen.
```

YOUR CORRECTED NOTE CARD:

```
Fraser 197

Those who favored the former Queen noticed
and were heartened by signs of friction
between Henry and Anne.
```

---

*APA-based material in exercises 89 and 90 copyright © 2001 by the American Psychological Association. Adapted with permission.

1. [From page 334 of a book by Walter Cronkite titled *A Reporter's Life*]

ORIGINAL: He [Daniel Ellsberg] had worked on the Pentagon's detailed history of our involvement in the Vietnam War. He became so incensed over what he considered the dirty secrets therein that he made off with hundreds of pages of papers and offered them to the news media.

STUDENT:

Cronkite, chap. 7

Daniel Ellsberg, who had worked on the Pentagon's involvement in Vietnam, became incensed over the dirty secrets he found and stole hundreds of papers, which he offered to the news media.

2. [From page 2 of an anonymous online article from the Sierra Club, "Endangered Species and Their Habitats"; last update, 4 Nov. 1995, retrieved 8 May 2003]

ORIGINAL: In fact, it is massive overcutting—along with automation and the industry's practice of exporting logs for processing with cheap, non-U.S. labor—that has wiped out over 90 percent of America's ancient forests.

STUDENT:

Sierra Club 2

"Massive overcutting" has caused the destruction of nine-tenths of our old-growth forests.

3. [From page 1319 of an article in the October 29, 1998, issue of the *New England Journal of Medicine*. The article is "Therapeutic Strategies for HIV Infection—Time to Think Hard" by David A. Cooper and Sean Emery. You may need a dictionary to rephrase medical jargon.]

ORIGINAL: We must think hard about the implications and practicalities of a medical strategy based on aggressive early intervention with lifelong, complex regimens of antiretroviral therapy to preserve immunocompetence after the suppression of a cytopathic virus.

STUDENT:

Emery, p. 1319

We must think hard about the implications and practical effects of a medical approach based on early aggressive intervening with "lifelong, complex regimens of antiretroviral therapy to preserve immuno-competence" after a cytopathic virus is suppressed.

4. [From a newspaper article by Jane Brody on page 18 of section A of the late edition of the *New York Times* of 6 September 2002. The article is "U.S. Panel Urges Hour of Exercise Each Day."]

ORIGINAL: As for carbohydrates, there is again a wide range of recommended intakes—45 to 65 percent of calories—to allow for dietary flexibility. This range recognizes that both the high-carbohydrate, low-fat diet of many Asian peoples and the higher-fat diet of Mediterranean peoples . . . are . . . associated with good health.

STUDENT:

Good health

When you eat carbohydrates, a wide range of intakes is recommended, from half to 3/4 of your calories. This gives your diet flexibility. This range takes into account that high fat Asian diets and low fat Mediterranean diets both lead to good health.

5. [From page 13 of a book by Philip Zelikow and Condoleezza Rice titled *Germany Unified and Europe Transformed: A Study in Statecraft*, published in 1995. (Gorbachev was the leader of the Soviet Union.)]

ORIGINAL: By far the most important man in Gorbachev's entourage was, like him, an outsider, with no foreign policy expertise. Eduard Shevardnadze, the foreign minister, had been too young to serve in World War II. . . .

STUDENT:

Rice and Zelikov 1995

It is my belief that both Gorbachev and his foreign minister, Eduard Shevardnadze, had very little experience in foreign policy. Shevardnadze had been even too young for World War II military service.

Write the material from each of your note cards in part 1, as you would write it in an actual research paper. Use MLA or APA style as indicated, or as your instructor directs. Be accurate, cite correctly, and do not plagiarize.

Example (MLA): According to Fraser, those who favored the former Queen noticed and were heartened by signs of friction between Henry and Anne (197).

1. (MLA) _____
_____
_____
_____
_____
_____

2. (MLA) _____
_____
_____
_____
_____
_____

3. (APA) _____
_____
_____
_____
_____
_____

4. (APA) _____
_____
_____
_____
_____
_____

5. (MLA) _____
_____
_____
_____
_____
_____

90. PARAGRAPHS AND PAPERS: The Works Cited/Reference List

(Study 509, The Works Cited/Reference List)

(Open book) Write a **correct** bibliographical entry for each item. Use **MLA** or **APA** style, or both, as your instructor directs. (If both, make a copy of this page before starting, or use your own paper, for the APA entries.) Your instructor may specify the COS alternative. In some items, more information may be given than is needed.

Example (MLA): Book: The Essential Heart Book for Women, by Morris Notelovitz and Diana Tonnessen, published in New York in 1996 by St. Martin's Griffin Press.

Notelovitz, Morris, and Diana Tonnessen. <u>The Essential Heart Book for Women</u>. New York: St. Martin's, 1996.

1. Book: Hateship, Friendship, Courtship, Loveship, Marriage. Author: Alice Munro. Published: 2001 by Alfred A. Knopf in New York.

   _____

   _____

   _____

   _____

2. Journal article: Therapeutic Strategies for HIV Infection—Time to Think Hard. Authors: David A. Cooper and Sean Emery. Journal: New England Journal of Medicine. Published: October 29, 1998, on pages 1319–1321 (pages consecutive throughout volume) of volume 339, number 18.

   _____

   _____

   _____

   _____

3. Online article by Linda Greenhouse in the New York Times Online. It is entitled Citizens' Rights: Justices Ban Two-Tiered Welfare. It was in the issue of May 18, 1999, and was retrieved (accessed) on June 3, 2000. There are no page or edition numbers. The Web address is http://www.nytimes.com/library/politics/scotus/articles/051899welfare-benefits.html.

   _____

   _____

   _____

   _____

4. Encyclopedia article: Title: Honoré de Balzac [a writer]. No author of article given. Published on pages 851–852 of vol. 1 of The New Encyclopaedia Britannica: Micropaedia, 15th edition. The publisher is Encyclopaedia Britannica, Inc., of Chicago, and the date is 1998.

_____

_____

_____

_____

5. Magazine article: Going Her Own Way. Author: Candace Ord Manroe. Magazine: Better Homes and Gardens. Published: September 2002 on pages 49–58 of volume 80, number 9.

_____

_____

_____

_____

6. Online article from personal Web site: Article title: The Mythic Role of Space Fiction. Name of site: Welcome from Sylvia Engdahl. Author: Sylvia Engdahl. Written August 17, 1998. No pages. No publishing organization given. Retrieved September 30, 2002. Web address: http://www.teleport.com/~sengdahl/spacemyth.htm

_____

_____

_____

_____

7. Newspaper article: Title: Talks on Global Warming Treaty Resuming Today. Author: John H. Cushman, Jr. Published on page 6 of section A of the late edition of the New York Times on November 2, 1998.

_____

_____

_____

_____

8. Compact disk: Title: Overtures. Composer: Ludwig van Beethoven. Performed by the Philharmonia Orchestra conducted by Otto Klemperer. Recorded by EMI Records of Hayes Middlesex, England, in 1990.

_____

_____

_____

_____

9. Story in collection: Story title: Girls Like You. Author: Jennifer Moses. Collection title: New Stories from the South: The Year's Best, 1998. Editor of collection: Shannon Ravenel. Story on pages 143–152 of collection. Collection published by Algonquin Books of Chapel Hill, Chapel Hill, North Carolina, in 1998.

_____

_____

_____

_____

10. Book: Title: Germany Unified and Europe Transformed: A Study in Statecraft. Authors: Philip Zelikow and Condoleezza Rice. Published in 1995 by the Harvard University Press in Cambridge, Massachusetts.

_____

_____

_____

_____

91. REVIEW: Proofreading

(Study 201–314, Punctuation; Mechanics, with Spelling)

Proofread the following paragraphs for **typographical errors, omitted** or **doubled words,** and errors in **punctuation, capitalization, number form, abbreviations,** and **spelling.** (You may use a dictionary.) Make all corrections neatly above the line.

(Collaborative option: Students work in pairs to detect and correct errors.)

1. It all began when I joined the U.S. Army. My atittude toward life changed completely. I had just truned twenty one and in the prime of my life. I had every thing, that I had always wanted when I was a Teenager. My parents had given me: no responsibiity, no realistic outlook on life and no understanding of what it meant to go form a small country town into a huge army Camp.

2. I came to know what predjudice really means when I was 11 yrs. old. I when with my family to a motel in Bleakville called the Welcome House motel. The clerk at the registration desk said to my Father "you're wife and children can stay here, but you cant. My sisters and I could'nt figure out why my father was being refused a room, untill my mother told us it was because he was a little darker then we were. I remember that the clock said eight-o-two p.m. There was no place else in town to stay, but we all picked up our bags and marched out of the Welcome House Motel.

3. The word grammer strikes fear or loathing into some student's hearts, but, such need not be the case. Its concepts can be simplifyed. For example take the 8 parts of speech; If you except Interjections which are grammatically unconnected to the rest of the sentence there are only four kinds of words; naming words (nouns), doing-being words (verbs), modifiers (adjs. and advs.) and connectors [prepositions and conjunctions.]

4. Ebbets field, home of the famed Brooklyn Dodgers baseball team is today hallowed in the memorys of of many as the perfect old ballpark—the ideal place to watch a game—. Though this small Stadium fell victim to the wreckers ball about fifty year's ago, after the Summer of nineteen fifty-seven it can still generate spasms of nostalgia in true baseball buffs. Actually, it was a dumpy old place with miserable parking, uncomfortable seats, poles that blocked ones view, inadequate lighting, and facilities were by today's standards decidedly primitive.

5.   Darlene gazed lovingley at Michael. "Oh, Michael I can't bear the though that you have to leave", she whispered. "must you go back to So. Hadleyville so soon."

"It's a 2 & one half hour trip," Michael replied. "and a snowstorm is blowing in from the North."

"If you go there is my ring!" she cried, pulling the gold band from her finger, and hurling it to the floor.

Michael wondered whether she was serious?

92. REVIEW: Editing and Proofreading

(Study 101–404: Grammar and Sentences; Punctuation; Mechanics, with Spelling; Word Choice)

Edit and proofread the paragraphs below. Look not only for **mechanical errors** as in exercise 91, but also for **weak or faulty sentence structure**, and for **grammatical** and **word-choice errors**. Use standard, formal English. Rewrite the paragraphs on your own paper.

(Collaborative option: Students work in pairs to detect and correct errors and weaknesses; students critique each other's rewrites.)

1. The birth of my son changed my whole life I found myself for the first time responsable for another human being. Because of complications in my pregnancy, I had to have a Cesarean, but everything work out without to much difficulty. Since then Roger has made me forget that pain. Being a healthy boy of five today, I find him a joy, even thorough he can occasionally be annoying. Everyone of his friends have a delightful time when playing with him. Because he has such a sunny disposition. Whenever a new child moved into the neighborhood, Roger is the first to run over and offer them his toys to play with.

2. The high pay earned by many athletes are ruining professional sports. These jerks are being paid outrageous amounts of money just to run around a field or a court for a few months. For example, Alex Rodriguez, the Yankee's star, was given a $250 million contract, and LeBron James will earn more than he can ever count. Most players' salarys exceed a million dollars. In baseball, ever since the players became free agents, they have recieved exorbitant paychecks. I believe such sums are being award to the players without regard to us fans. How many of us can afford to pay a price that amounts to a total of $100 for a seat at a basketball game. Moreover, the players are rarely exerting maximum effort to justify their seven-figure incomes. I, for one, will not return back to Municipal Stadium or Central Coliseum unless they have scheduled a good college game there. It is up to we fans to reverse this thing by boycotting professional games.

3. Most Americans are woefully ignorant of the World's geography. Where a country is located, what kind of resources does it have, and how far away it is are questions that bring a puzzled frown to many? Angola, for example. Where is it? Is it an island? What do they produce there? What are it's people like, do they think and act like we do? Just because a land is distant from us doesn't mean that it's not importent. Being so far from our shores, Americans should not ignore other countries.

4. Commuting to a city College from your home may seem less attractive then to live on a rolling green campus in the hills. Yet they have many advantages. Lower cost is an obvious one, home cooked meals is another. It gives a student the freedom to go wherever they want after classes: to movies or shows, museums, or even get a part-time job. Citys are full of exciting places to find excitement in, therefore they form a welcome antidote for boring classes.

5. There are a right way and a wrong way to walk when hiking. First of all, stay relaxed and no slouching. Swing you're arms, this will help relaxation and momentum it will also make you feel good. You should maintain straightness in your shoulders & hips to. When carrying a pack, leaning a bit forward will help a person center their weight over their feet. Carry plenty of water, and stop to rest after a half an hour.

93. REVIEW: Revising, Editing, and Proofreading

(Study 101–503: Grammar and Sentences; Punctuation; Mechanics, with Spelling; Word Choice; Paragraphs)

On your own paper, **revise**, **edit**, and **proofread** the paragraphs below. Correct **all errors** and make any necessary **improvements**, including strengthening **paragraph structure**. Use all the skills and knowledge you have learned in *English Simplified.*

(Collaborative option: Students work in pairs to detect and correct errors and weaknesses; students critique each other's rewrites.)

1. The government must take strong action against polluters, they are slowly killing us all. By poisoning our air and our water. The big business lobbies control Congress, and so it passes few antipollution laws. Its frightening, for example to find that Midwest smokestacks fill the air with acid. Rain becomes filled with this acid. It is killing fish in Adirondack Mountain lakes. These lakes are hundreds of miles to the east. Elsewhere, pesticides are being used. They are being sprayed on potato fields. The chemicals seep underground, and then the local well water becomes contaminated. In Texas, polluted water almost killed ten thousand cattle. The corpses of these cattle had to be burned to prevent the spread of the poison. The government is responding far too weak to this pollution crisis. Congress must resist the lobbyists, and strong antipollution laws must be passed by it.

2. "Warning: The surgion general has determined that cigarette smoking is dangerous to your health," or a similar message printed on all packs of cigaretes but people still smoke. Did you ever wonder why? Every smoker know that cigarettes are harmful to their lungs, but this doesn't stop them. I believe that people just don't care any more about their selves. Years ago people they tried to live longer and not to do any thing that would damage their health now things have changed. I feel that people feel that their is nothing to live for and if your going to die it has to be from something even if its not cancer. Also people relizing that life is not to easy. Price's are going up jobs are hard to find and who wants to live in a world where many things are difficult to get. Being a non smoker myself, cigarettes should be banned from society. If they were baned from society, smokers will live longer. In spite of themself.

3. Enlisting in the army was an experience that changed my life. June 10, 2001 was the day it began. The plane left Boston for Georgia. The plane arrived three hours later. A group of us recruits waited for four more hours for the bus to come to take us to Ft. Gordon. The bus came and took us to camp. We were processed in and given sleeping quarters. They were cold and drafty. The first week was spent in a reception center. It was nice there, too nice. The next week we were transfered to our duty stations to start the armys new basic training program. The sergents appeared to look nice but that was just a dream, For five weeks we did the same grueling thing everyday. At four o'clock we woke up, did lots of exercises, etc, and did the things that had to be done that day. The training was easy but the sergent's made it hard. Some of the other guys were there made it worst. They resisted the discipline. The last week had come and I was a new person. I have learned that, I will never join anything with out thinking twice about it.

4. Cross-country skiing is not as popular as downhill skiing. But it has been slowly but steadily gaining in popularity in the United States, and this is a good thing because it is a much more aerobic sport that is, it gives the skier a better cardiovascular workout and is therefore better for your all-around health, which, in turn, can lead to a person having a longer life. Cross-country skiing will burn up to 9 hundred calories an hour, moreover the upper body muscles are developed as well as the lower body, which is the only part that running or cycling develop. Beside this it developes coordination. And they have less risk of injury then downhill skiers.

5. One of the biggest dangers in writing a paragraph is straying from the topic. Our history professor does this often when lecturing. Another is fused sentences they sneak up on you, so do comma splices. By dangling a modifier, your composition can sound silly. Do not shift voice or mood, for your essay can be made confusing by it. Lack of agreement between subjects and verbs reveal a careless writer at work. Worst of all is to have no topic sentence or cohesion.

94. ACHIEVEMENT TEST: Grammar, Sentences, and Paragraphs

Part 1: Sentences

Write **S** if the boldfaced expression is one complete, correct **sentence**.
Write **F** if it is a **fragment** (incorrect: less than a complete sentence).
Write **Spl** or **FS** if it is a **comma splice** or **fused sentence** (incorrect: two or more sentences written as one).

Example: The climbers suffered from hypothermia. **Having neglected to bring warm clothing.**   ____F____

1. Senator Wanhope won a stunning victory. **After trailing badly in nearly every pre-election poll.**   1. _____

2. The nation's airlines are instituting stricter security measures. **Such as arming pilots, securing cockpit doors, and placing plainclothes federal marshals aboard most flights.**   2. _____

3. **He will attend college his high school grades are good enough.**   3. _____

4. The rancher sold most of his livestock. **Then he turned his property into a profitable dude ranch.**   4. _____

5. **Elated at news of the victory.** Borrelli broke out a bottle of her finest champagne.   5. _____

6. **When does abstract art become just scribbles?**   6. _____

7. **Our guests having arrived, we sat down to dinner.**   7. _____

8. Nine families joined the pollution study. **They will wear carbon-filter badges, this device will monitor the air that they are breathing.**   8. _____

9. **The storm having washed out the bridge.** We had to spend the night in town.   9. _____

10. Sir Thisby invited me to play cricket. **A game I had never even watched.**   10. _____

11. **The high humidity forced us to move the picnic inside it was just too hot to eat outside.**   11. _____

12. **The student who tape-records the physics lecture.**   12. _____

13. **I continued to watch the baseball game on television even though I had not started my calculus homework that was due the next day.**   13. _____

14. Allen used a week's vacation. **To sand and refinish the hardwood floors in his home.**   14. _____

15. **Children in the experimental group improved their reading scores by nearly a full grade, however, six-month follow-up studies showed that the gains did not last.**   15. _____

16. **Though armed and considered dangerous, he surrendered without a struggle.**   16. _____

Part 2: Grammar

In the blank, write **C** if the boldfaced expression is used **correctly**.
Write **X** if it is used **incorrectly**.

Example: There **was** dozens of dinosaur bones on the site.   ____X____

1. It was a personal matter between Terry and **myself**.   1. _____

2. During the summer, she trained horses, **which** assisted her financially.   2. _____

3. At the building supply store there **were** insulation, sheet rock, and flashing.

3. _____

4. Cousin Max, along with his twin daughters and their cats, **were** waiting at my front door.

4. _____

5. The interviewer asked each of the politicians to explain **their** position on taxation.

5. _____

6. Copies of *Esquire* and *Rolling Stone* **was** in Dr. Moore's waiting room.

6. _____

7. The taxi driver gave Tony and **I** a scornful glance.

7. _____

8. The ticket agent gave Ed and **me** seats that were behind home plate.

8. _____

9. Every committee member **was** given a copy of the report.

9. _____

10. **Refusing to pay high interest**, consumers are cutting up their credit cards.

10. _____

11. Parking restrictions apply **not only** to students **but also** to visitors.

11. _____

12. His mother wanted him to become a corporate lawyer. **This** kept Leonard in college.

12. _____

13. Students should meet their professors, so that if **you** have questions about class, **you** will feel comfortable approaching a professor during office hours.

13. _____

14. **Having an hour to kill,** there was time to stroll through the village.

14. _____

15. His plans included landing a well-paying internship and **to spend** as much time as possible with his girlfriend.

15. _____

16. **Being nervous about the speech**, the microphone amplified my quavering voice.

16. _____

17. We wondered why the list of courses **was** not posted yet.

17. _____

18. There are few people who write in a personal journal as much as **her**.

18. _____

19. I like swimming in icy lakes as well as **to relax in the warm sunshine**.

19. _____

20. Aggression **is when** one nation attacks another without provocation.

20. _____

21. **Is** either of the two bands ready to go on?

21. _____

22. Was it you **who** wrote the editorial titled "Ban Smoking on Campus"?

22. _____

23. Everyone who plays the lottery hopes that **their** ticket will win the million-dollar jackpot.

23. _____

24. It is up to **us** freshmen to demand better food in the dining hall.

24. _____

25. All of **we** residents living in the Sussex area were upset when a fast-food restaurant was built nearby.

25. _____

26. Financial aid will be made available to **whoever** shows a need for it.

26. _____

27. Every student should understand that it is up to **you** to find the strategies to do well academically.

27. _____

28. He coached Little League and joined two service clubs. **It** was expected of him by his associates.

28. _____

29. Harry and **myself** solved the crime of the missing coffee pot in the lounge.

29. _____

30. **Who** do you think will apply for the position of dean of students?

30. _____

31. There **was** a Buick, a Toyota, and a Mercedes parked in the lot.

31. _____

32. Between you and **I**, Martin has only a slim chance of promotion this year.

32. _____

33. **Is** there any objections to your opening a nightclub on campus?

33. _____

34. My advisor suggested that I take Russian. **That** was fine with me.

34. _____

35. Each of the players **has** two passes for all home games.

35. _____

36. Neither Joan nor her two attendants **was** asked to appear on television.

36. _____

37. He is one of the engineering students who **are** interning this summer.   37. _____

38. You will never find anyone more responsible than **her**.   38. _____

39. Jenette is the **friendliest** of the two resident assistants in my building.   39. _____

40. When the Buffalo Bills and the Pittsburgh Steelers play, I know **they** will win.   40. _____

41. Why not give the keys to **whomever** you think will be in charge?   41. _____

42. Did the committee approve of **his** assuming the chair position?   42. _____

43. The study **not only** disproved Blunt's theory **but also** McDavid's.   43. _____

44. In his backpack **were** a notebook computer, an umbrella, and his lunch; he was prepared for a
day on campus.   44. _____

45. The coach, as well as the manager and players, **was** sure of winning.   45. _____

46. **Knowing of his parents' disapproval**, it seemed wise for him to reconsider his plan to drop
out of school to become a skydiving instructor.   46. _____

47. Daniel decided to **only** purchase three new fish for his aquarium.   47. _____

48. If he **were** more tactful, he would have fewer enemies.   48. _____

49. **If you submit your paper late** does not mean that it will be graded *F*.   49. _____

50. Neither the camp director nor the hikers **was** aware of their danger.   50. _____

Part 3: Paragraphs (not included in scoring)

In the space below or on the back, write a **paragraph** of six to eight sentences on **one** of the following topics (you may use scrap paper also):

_____

The thrill of _____ (something you have done)

A friend I will never forget

If I could go on television for five minutes

The best (or worst) book I have read in the past year

A sorely needed law

95. ACHIEVEMENT TEST: Punctuation

Write **C** if the punctuation in brackets is **correct**.
Write **X** if it is **incorrect**.
(Use only one number in each blank.)

Example: Regular exercise[,] and sound nutrition are essential for good health.   ___X___

1. Santee, South Carolina[,] is the site of a huge outlet mall.   1. _____

2. Residents[,] who own barking dogs[,] refuse to do anything about the noise.   2. _____

3. He thought the idea was mine, but it was their[']s.   3. _____

4. The strike having been averted[,] the workers returned to their jobs.   4. _____

5. He asked me where I had bought my surfboard[?]   5. _____

6. When I open it[']s favorite cat food, the cat races into the kitchen.   6. _____

7. Haven't you often heard it said, "Haste makes waste["?]   7. _____

8. Wouldn't you like to go to the rally with us?"[,] asked the girl across the hall.   8. _____

9. He said, "Let's walk across the campus.[" "]It's such a warm evening."   9. _____

10. Enrollment is up to three[-]thousand students this quarter.   10. _____

11. Twenty[-]six students have volunteered to serve on various committees.   11. _____

12. Dear Sir[;] I have enclosed my application and résumé.   12. _____

13. After you have finished your sociology assignment[,] let's go to a movie.   13. _____

14. Billy Budd struck Claggart[;] because he could not express himself any other way.   14. _____

15. You did agree to give the presentation[,] didn't you?   15. _____

16. We were early[;] as a matter of fact, we were first among the guests to arrive.   16. _____

17. "If you really look closely," the art critic commented[,] "you'll see a purple turtle in the middle of the painting."   17. _____

18. Dr. Johnson had little praise for the current health care system[;] calling it an elitist structure.   18. _____

19. The band recorded its first album in the spring[,] and followed it with a summer concert tour.   19. _____

20. She had hoped to arrange a two month[']s tour of Korea and Japan.   20. _____

21. We hope[,] Ms. Foster[,] that your office will be satisfactory.   21. _____

22. The next stockholders' meeting is scheduled for August 9, 2007[,] but it will be open only to major investors.   22. _____

23. My youngest sister[,] who is fourteen[,] is already shopping for a college.   23. _____

24. Because she played cards until midnight[;] she overslept.   24. _____

25. Jane Cox[,] a biochemistry major[,] won the top scholarship.   25. _____

26. Professor Thomas was asked to create a course for the Women[']s Studies Department.   26. _____

27. The little boy in the center of the old photograph[,] would later write five novels.   27. _____

28. "As for who has written the winning essay[—]well, I haven't as yet heard from the judges," said Mr. Hawkins.

28. _____

29. What he described about the massive oil spill[,] filled us with horror.

29. _____

30. I asked Elizabeth what we should do about our vacation plans[?]

30. _____

31. The newly elected officers are Denzell Jones, president[;] Ruby Pillsbury, vice president[;] and Maria Garcia, secretary.

31. _____

32. Before the radical group surrendered[;] they attempted to negotiate their freedom.

32. _____

33. We followed the trail over several ridges[,] and along the edge of two mountain lakes.

33. _____

34. Before touring Europe, I had many matters to attend to[;] such as making reservations, buying clothes, and getting a passport.

34. _____

35. Having a good sense of humor helps one put problems into perspective[;] certainly it's better than brooding.

35. _____

36. The ticket agent inquired ["]if we were planning to stop in Paris.["]

36. _____

37. Once retired, Ensel painted portraits of family pets[,] and played bingo every Thursday and Saturday.

37. _____

38. Marcia learned that all foods[,] which are high in fat[,] should be eaten in moderation.

38. _____

39. We were told to read ["]Ode to a Nightingale,["] a poem by Keats.

39. _____

40. The alumni magazine had a column cleverly entitled ["]Grad-Tidings.["]

40. _____

41. A civilian conservation corps could provide[:] education, training, and work for thousands of unemployed teenagers.

41. _____

42. Some people wish to have ["]America, the Beautiful["] become our national anthem.

42. _____

43. She hurried towards us[,] her books clasped under her arm[,] to tell us the good news.

43. _____

44. The audience wanted him to sing one more song[;] however, he refused.

44. _____

45. They must be the only ones who have visited New York in recent years and not seen the show ["]The Lion King[."]

45. _____

46. She found a note in her mailbox: "Sorry to have missed you. The Lawson[']s."

46. _____

47. His mother wanted him to major in chemistry[;] he wanted to major in music.

47. _____

48. Chris decided that he wanted a quiet vacation[,] not one full of schedules and guided tours.

48. _____

49. He had gone to the library[. B]ecause he wanted to borrow some videos.

49. _____

50. Her program included courses in English[,] social science[,] and chemistry.

50. _____

51. Every child knows "Twinkle, twinkle, little star[/]How I wonder what you are."

51. _____

52. To prepare for the baseball tryouts[,] Sam practiced every night.

52. _____

53. Ms. Whitney, who is a physical education instructor, came to the rally[;] with Mr. Martin, who is the football coach.

53. _____

54. When the tornado hit eastern Ohio[,] it caused millions of dollars of damage.

54. _____

55. "Some of the seniors wer[']ent able to pay their dues," she said.

55. _____

56. Frank Anderson[,] who is on the tennis team[,] is an excellent athlete.

56. _____

57. "All motorists[,] who fail to stop at the crosswalk[,] should be put in jail!" declared an angry parent.

57. _____

58. Looking at me sweetly, Mark replied, "No[,] I will not lend you a thousand dollars."

58. _____

59. George enrolled in a course in home economics; Elsa[,] in woodworking.   59. _____

60. "Haven't I met you somewhere before?"[,] he asked.   60. _____

61. "It's most unlikely["!] she said, turning away.   61. _____

62. A student[,] whom I met at the banquet[,] would like to work in our department next semester.   62. _____

63. It is a monumental task to build a highway[,] where 10,000-foot mountains block the way.   63. _____

64. He moved to Denver[,] where he worked as a freelance photographer.   64. _____

65. We were[,] on the other hand[,] not surprised by his decision.   65. _____

66. I bought a special type of paintbrush to reach those hard[-]to[-]reach spots near the rain gutters.   66. _____

67. Listen to the arguments of both speakers[,] then decide which side you favor.   67. _____

68. Four generations of Spencer[']s will attend the family reunion.   68. _____

69. Susannah is familiar with many customs of Sweden [(]her father's homeland[)] and can prepare many Swedish dishes.   69. _____

70. Our ex[-]mayor pleaded guilty to a speeding ticket.   70. _____

71. The conference sponsored by our fraternity was successful[,] especially the sessions concerning community-service projects.   71. _____

72. The Liberty scored ten points in the last minute but[,] the Sparks held on for the win.   72. _____

73. Jack displayed a unique [(?)] talent when he created a collage of spaghetti sauce, pickles, and pancakes.   73. _____

74. The children[,] on the other hand[,] were content to wear last year's coats and boots.   74. _____

75. The teenager used the word [*like*] throughout her conversation.   75. _____

96. ACHIEVEMENT TEST: Mechanics, Spelling, and Word Choice

Part 1: Capitalization

In each blank, write **C** if the boldfaced word(s) **follow** the rules of capitalization.
Write **X** if the word(s) **do not follow** the rules.

Example: The Mormons settled in what is now **Salt Lake City**.   _____C_____

1. Please meet Charles Ebbings, **Professor** of psychology at Yale.   1. _____
2. It was relaxing to spend a few days away from **college**.   2. _____
3. She is **President** of her class.   3. _____
4. I belong to a **Science Club.**   4. _____
5. He plays for Ohio **State**.   5. _____
6. We saluted the **american** flag.   6. _____
7. We flew over the **french Alps**.   7. _____
8. I asked **Grandmother** to lend me the family album.   8. _____
9. He enjoys living in the **Southwest**.   9. _____
10. The **East** side of the house needs to be repainted.   10. _____
11. I visited an **indian** village while on vacation.   11. _____
12. He naps in his **history** class.   12. _____
13. We heard that **Aunt Harriet** had eloped with the butcher.   13. _____
14. The note began, "My **Dear** John."   14. _____
15. I am going to be a **Medical Anthropologist**.   15. _____
16. The magazine recommended buying a Dell **Computer**.   16. _____
17. I lost points because the answer key contained an error; **nevertheless**, Professor Pruyn refused
    to change my grade.   17. _____
18. History 303 studies the Russian **Revolution**.   18. _____
19. We toured the lakes and woodlands where the novel *The Last Of The Mohicans* took place.   19. _____
20. Walter prayed that **god** would let him win the lottery.   20. _____

Part 2: Abbreviations and Numbers

Write **C** if the boldfaced abbreviation or number is used **correctly**.
Write **X** if it is used **incorrectly**.

Example: They drove through **Tenn.**   <u>   X   </u>

1. **Fifty million** voters stayed away from the polls.   1. _____
2. Thank God it's **Fri**.   2. _____
3. My cat named Holiday is **5**.   3. _____
4. We live on Sutherland **Rd**.   4. _____
5. She was born on July **6th**, 1980.   5. _____
6. Please meet me at **10** o'clock.   6. _____
7. He released **two hundred** pigeons at the picnic.   7. _____
8. After a brief investigation, we discovered that **13** students were involved in the prank.   8. _____
9. The train leaves at **8** p.m.   9. _____
10. Dinner was served at **six** o'clock.   10. _____
11. Joan Allen, **Ph.D.,** spoke first.   11. _____
12. Lunch cost **12** dollars!   12. _____
13. **Ms**. Martin, please chair the meeting today.   13. _____
14. Lloyd's monthly salary is now **$3,200.50**.   14. _____
15. They lived at **six seventy-four** Ninth Avenue.   15. _____

Part 3: Spelling

In each sentence, one boldfaced word is **misspelled**. Write its number in the blank.

Example: (1)**Its** (2)**too** late (3)**to** go.   <u>   1   </u>

1. Horace's (1)**peculiar** expression of boredom was his way of making a (2)**statment** about the quality of the (3)**equipment**.   1. _____
2. The open (1)**cemetary** gates permitted an (2)**excellent** (3)**opportunity** for Karloff's laboratory assistant.   2. _____
3. My (1)**psychology** (2)**proffessor** assigns a weekly (3)**written** report.   3. _____
4. He needed (1)**permission** from the (2)**commitee** to participate in the (3)**competition**.   4. _____
5. The (1)**bookkeeper** learned that a (2)**knowledge** of (3)**grammer** is helpful.   5. _____
6. A (1)**fourth** such disaster threatens the very (2)**existance** of the Alaskan (3)**environment.**   6. _____
7. Arthur (1)**definately** considered it a (2)**privilege** to help write the (3)**article**.   7. _____
8. The (1)**principal** (2)**complimented** her for her (3)**excellant** performance.   8. _____
9. It was (1)**apparent** that she was (2)**desparate** because she was listening to his (3)**advice**.   9. _____
10. We (1)**imediately** became (2)**familiar** with the requirements for a (3)**license**.   10. _____
11. Is it (1)**permissable** to ask him to (2)**recommend** me for a (3)**government** position?   11. _____

12. (1)**Personaly**, I didn't believe his (2)**analysis** of the result of the (3)**questionnaire**.   12._____

13. The test pilot felt enormous (1)**optimism** after her third (2)**repitition** of the dangerous (3)**maneuver**.   13._____

14. It's (1)**ridiculus** that Sue became so angry about the (2)**criticism** of her friend, the (3)**playwright**.   14._____

15. She was not (1)**conscious** of being (2)**unnecessarily** (3)**persistant** about the matter.   15._____

Part 4: Word Choice

To be correct, the boldfaced expression must be standard, formal English and must not be sexist or otherwise discriminatory.
Write **C** if the boldfaced word is used **correctly**.
Write **X** if it is used **incorrectly**.

Examples: The counsel's **advice** was misinterpreted.   <u>   C   </u>
           They **could of** made the plane except for the traffic.   <u>   X   </u>

1. I was not **altogether** amused.   1._____

2. Aaron looked **sort of** tired after the test.   2._____

3. They are all old; for **instants**, Grayson is eighty-six.   3._____

4. Billy cried when his balloon **burst**.   4._____

5. Next time, plan to invite **fewer** guests.   5._____

6. He earned no interest on his **principal**.   6._____

7. **Can** I add your name as a contributor to the scholarship fund?   7._____

8. The judge would hear no **farther** arguments.   8._____

9. I am in real trouble, **aren't I**?   9._____

10. The team was **plenty** angry.   10._____

11. The parent **persuaded** her child to take out the garbage.   11._____

12. He notified **most** of his creditors.   12._____

13. She knows **less** people than I.   13._____

14. Saul made an **illusion** to *Hamlet*.   14._____

15. Was the murderer **hanged**?   15._____

16. The team **would of** done much better with a different quarterback.   16._____

17. The **kids** were excited.   17._____

18. I had **already** signed the check.   18._____

19. John sounds **like** he needs a vacation.   19._____

20. I can't stand **those kind** of jokes.   20._____

21. He is **real** happy about winning the contest.   21._____

22. The cat is **lying** by the fire.   22._____

23. She **generally always** works hard.   23._____

261

24. He does **good** in math courses.   24. _____

25. His speech **implied** that he would raise taxes.   25. _____

26. We took the tour because of its awesome **things to see**.   26. _____

27. On the bus were city people, suburbanites, and **hillbillies**.   27. _____

28. The chair was about **thirty inches in width**.   28. _____

29. **Due to the fact of his escape**, the police have set up roadblocks.   29. _____

30. Our vacation was even **more perfect** than you can imagine.   30. _____

The following chart gives brief definitions and examples of the grammatical terms you will read about most often in these exercises. Refer to *English Simplified* for more information.

Term	**What It Is or Does**	**Examples**
Adjective	Describes a noun	a **fast** runner (describes the noun **runner**)
Appositive	A noun that renames another	Tom Wolfe, **the writer**, lives in New York. (The appositive follows the man's name.)
Adverb	Describes a verb, adjective, or another adverb	He runs **fast** (describes the verb **run**). He runs **very** fast (describes the adverb **fast**). He is an **extremely** fast runner (describes the adjective **fast**).
Clause	A group of words with a subject and a predicate. An independent clause can stand by itself and make complete sense; a dependent clause must be attached to an independent clause.	**He is a fast runner.** (An independent clause) **if he is a fast runner** (A dependent clause that must be attached to some independent clause, such as **He will win.**)
Complement	Completes the meaning of the verb	Direct Object: He threw the **ball.** (Says what was thrown.)
		Indirect Object: He threw **me** the ball. (Says to whom the ball was thrown.)
		Subjective Complement: He is a **pitcher.** (Renames the subject **He** after the linking verb **is.**)
		Objective Complement: The team named Rodgers **coach.** (Follows the direct object **Rodgers** and renames it.)
Conjunction	A word that joins	Coordinating Conjunction: Joins things of equal importance: Men **and** women. Poor **but** honest.
		Subordinating Conjunction: Joins a dependent clause to a main clause: I left **when** she arrived.
Fragment	A group of words that cannot stand by itself as a sentence	**when I saw them** (a dependent clause); **from Maine to California** (a prepositional phrase)
Noun	Names a person, place, animal, thing, or idea	**Tom, Denver, cat, book, love, truth**
Phrase	A group of related words without a subject and a verb	**from California** (a prepositional phrase); **to see the king** (an infinitive phrase); **built of bricks** (a participial phrase); **building houses** (a gerund phrase)
(Complete) Predicate	The part of the sentence that speaks about the subject	The man **threw the ball.** (says what the subject did)
Pronoun	A word that replaces a noun (or replaces a word group acting as a noun)	**He** will be here soon. (**He** takes the place of the man's name.)
Subject	The person or thing about whom the sentence speaks	**Polly** writes children's books.
Verb	Says what the subject either does or is	She **buys** seashells. She **is** a doctor.